Hands
Of A Teacher
The Alfreda Drummond Story

To the Johnsons:
Thanks for your friendship.
Best wishes.

Love,
Freda

Hands
Of A Teacher
The Alfreda Drummond Story

by
Alfreda L. A. Drummond

PUBLISHING CONNECTIONS

This book is dedicated
to the fond memories of my husbands,
Samuel S. Alexander Sr. and Willis R. Drummond Sr.,
and to my son, Samuel S. Alexander Jr. "Dickie,"
in recognition of the scholastic and work accomplishments
he has achieved and the joy and inspiration
he has provided others.

For information, write:
Publishing Connections
621 Hampton Highway
Yorktown, VA 23693
(757) 867-8287
E-mail address: pubconn@pilot.infi.net

Library of Congress Cataloging-in-Publication Data
Drummond, Alfreda L. A.
Hands of a Teacher: The Alfreda Drummond Story
Library of Congress Catalog Number: 97-75427
ISBN: 0-9643374-7-9

Publisher, Editor: Laura D. Hill
Senior Editor: Dr. Margaret Bristow
Art Director, Designer: Mary Beth Apperson

Printed in the United States of America

Table of Contents

Preface

At a very early age my parents told me I had "hands of a teacher" and that they would make a teacher out of me. I was so impressed! The statement "hands of a teacher" became an endless melody within my conscience. My heart would not let go of the melodic theme until the words became a reality. It would take twenty-two years of hard work, overcoming financial hurdles, and self determination before my parents' prophesy was fulfilled.

Hands of A Teacher: The Alfreda Drummond Story records the tragedies and triumphs of my journey to become a teacher. It begins with my early years sharecropping on North Carolina farms with my parents and seven brothers and sisters, and spans more than 60 years. The lifelong struggle to help support my family, to raise a son, and to further my education are captured on the following pages.

In 1964 my dream of becoming a teacher was realized. I earned a college degree from Hampton Institute in Hampton, Virginia, and began my professional teaching career at Thomas Jefferson Elementary School in Newport News, Virginia.

Over the next four years, I earned a Master's Degree in Education from Indiana University. I also completed additional graduate courses at the College of William and Mary, Old Dominion University, and the University of Virginia. In 1972 and 1977, I was promoted to Assistant Principal and Principal positions in the Newport News Public School System.

I am writing this book to share my experiences with others. I hope it will inspire adults and children to pursue their dreams. Unlimited opportunities await us when we refuse to give up the pursuit of our goals. Never surrender!

Alfreda L.A. Drummond
Retired Elementary Teacher and Principal

•

Acknowledgments

First, I thank God for His blessings and spiritual guidance throughout my life. Many people have given me encouragement and support over the years, which I have truly appreciated. I wish to express special gratitude to the following people:

My husband, the late Willis R. Drummond, Senior, who always said, "You can write the book. Go on and try."

My son, Dickie, who frequently asked, "When are you going to write the book?"

My brothers and sisters, who encouraged me to pursue higher achievements and assisted whenever there was a need.

Nancy Fenton, the former cafeteria manager at South Morrison Elementary School in Newport News, Virginia. When I retired, she told me she would be waiting to read my book.

Jerome Young, a family friend, motivated me to write by teasing me about starting college late, finishing early, getting to the top of my career fast, and retiring early.

Laura Hill of Publishing Connections, who helped me achieve my goals by offering research, consulting, and publishing expertise. Her professional guidance, friendly attitude, and feedback kept me on the right track.

William V.N. Requa encouraged me to write my memoirs to encourage people after he had read an article in the newspaper about me.

Reverend Dr. Lawrence Bethel, my pastor, suggested that I

write this book to become a mentor for children by encouraging them to become successful like me.

Lula Hardy, a former co-worker at Modern Cleaners, who threatened to place a can in a barber shop to collect money to send me to college and encouraged me to write this book.

Dr. Margaret Bristow and Mary Beth Apperson of Publishing Connections, who provided editing and design expertise.

•

Introduction

I have known Alfreda Drummond more than 40 years. Early into our relationship, I realized she was very special. Many of the experiences that she writes about in this book have been shared with me and others.

For many years Alfreda Drummond has expressed a desire to write her life story. Friends and family members have often encouraged her. Since I have been the beneficiary of much of her wisdom, optimism, humor, and love, I felt her story would be very entertaining and inspiring to others.

Over the years I have observed Alfreda Drummond's determination, hard work, concern for others, and efforts to do the right things. These attributes have enriched her life and the lives of so many people.

Like most young people, I grew up looking for a role model. In my quest, I did not have to look very far. For the author, Alfreda Drummond, is my mother. Writing this book has been a dream come true for her. I hope you will enjoy reading it as much as she has enjoyed sharing her story with you.

Samuel S. Alexander Jr.

part one

Childhood Memories

My father, Arterway Ben Lane, in the early 1940s.
A sharp dresser, he was the epitome of tall, dark, and handsome.
Photo from the author's collection.

●

chapter one

Family Tree

"Freda, I want you to come over here," Ma said as she pulled me into her bedroom. When I walked in I saw Daddy sitting on their bed holding a book on his lap. As I moved closer towards him, I noticed the pictures in the book showed different shapes of hands. Written below each set of hands was the occupation that the hands represented. Comparing my hands to those of a teacher they announced, "Your hands are shaped like the hands of a teacher. We're going to make a teacher out of you!" This statement was crystallized in my young mind and birthed a longing ambition within me to become a teacher.

My parents, Arterway and Lillie Willis Lane, were born in 1894 near Edgecomb County, North Carolina. There are one hundred counties in North Carolina. Edgecomb County, located on the Eastern coastal plain, was a farming community. The coastal plain is covered with forests of pine, pine tar, oak, magnolias, and walnut trees. Thus, people who live on the plain are called "tar hills" and North Carolina is known nationwide as the "Tar Hill State."

My father's full name was Arterway Ben Lane. He was one of six children born to Ben Lane, a sharecropper, and his wife, Mary.

Like most southern farm boys in the 1890s, Arterway attend-

My mother, Lillie Willis Lane, in 1926.
She was the chief disciplinarian, but even made discipline fun at times.
Photo from the author's collection.

ed grade school, but left school at a young age to work on the farm. Whatever he lacked in book knowledge, he made up for in hard work and good common sense.

Arterway's skin was rich brown, the shade of brown sugar. A sharp dresser, he grew to be five feet, ten inches tall and lean. The epitome of "tall, dark, and handsome," he was a man of many talents.

When he was not farming, he could be found fishing, hunting, trapping animals, and building chicken houses and smoke houses, which stored smoked meats from hogs. He also did house repairs and even made "home remedies" for the family. Arterway often made his talents available to friends and neighbors, who sought him out to repair their cars, sharpen hair clippers, repair shoe soles, and cut hair. He charged a small fee for these services, which meant he always had a "little money" in his pocket even during the Depression years of the 1920s and 1930s.

Although my father earned his living sharecropping, he studied to become an ordained Baptist minister. He never served as a pastor of a church, but he was a guest minister at several churches in Edgecomb County. He also became a skilled barber, giving him a marketable skill to fall back on when his sharecropping days ended.

One of my favorite memories of my father is that he was an excellent cook. He operated a small restaurant in Leggett, North Carolina when I was a baby. When he cooked dishes he would add spices or onions to make them taste different than my mother's. His spaghetti and meatballs was delicious. He made a scrumptious bread pudding by placing layers of loaf bread, raisins, sugar, butter, nutmeg and milk. It was then baked in a wooden stove. There were never any leftovers! I often equated excellent cooking with any food that looked different from my mother's.

My mother's full name was Orpha Lillie Willis. Fair complexioned, with a round face, long curly hair, and a petite frame, this beautiful woman stood about five feet, two inches tall.

Her father, owner of a large farm in Edgecomb County, was white. Although having a white father in the 1890s was not uncommon in the south, I never heard my my mother speak of her father. I never met him or knew his name.

My grandmother's name was Annie Willis. Annie had three sons. Lillie was her only daughter.

Lillie finished grade school and went on to complete high school at Brick Boarding School, which later became Brick Tri-County High School. It was the same school my sisters and I attended.

I only remember one of my grandparents—Ben Lane. I called him "Grandpopper." He looked just like Daddy, but was a little shorter and a bit chubby. Grandpopper lived in Edgecomb County, too, and visited frequently. Grandpopper always brought me candy from the country store.

During the 1920s, millions of southern sharecroppers left the farms and moved to large northern cities in hopes of enjoying a better life. Working on the farms required twelve to thirteen hour work days. In the northern cities the average work day was eight hours and the pay was greater. This caused my uncles to move to New York at an early age. So I seldom saw them.

Both of my grandmothers died before I was old enough to have any memories of them. During the Depression years, some people could rarely afford to go to the doctor. When they were sick, neighbors would come over to pray and sit with them. Sometimes they just watched them die. Both of my grandmothers died at an early age. Grandma Mary Lane died in her early 30s and Grandpopper remarried a woman named Susie. We called her Aunt Susie because she was so young. Grandma Annie died in 1924, the same year I was born.

My mother had more education than most farm women, but I only remember her working on the farm and raising children. Like most mothers during 1920s and 1930s, Lillie was respon-

Daddy holding me in 1925. I was about a year old.
My mother said I had been fussy that day, so Daddy took me out to
have my picture taken. *Photo from the author's collection.*

sible for all the household chores. She taught me to cook, sew, wash, iron, make up beds, can, and preserve foods.

Lillie was a great mother. I often thought of her as a "pal." She had a good sense of humor and a hearty laugh. Hearing her joyful laugh often made me laugh.

Although she enjoyed having fun with us, my mother was the chief disciplinarian. But she even made discipline fun at times. For thirteen years my brother, Bernard (Buddy), was the only boy amongst six sisters. Whenever he misbehaved, he would run from her. Then she would ask the girls to try to catch him. While we were chasing Buddy, she would stand there watching us, laughing. That was the end of Buddy's punishment!

Like my father, Lillie was industrious. In addition to sharecropping, she made most of our clothes. I would browse through Speigel catalogs to find pictures of dresses I liked. My mother would take the pictures and use newspapers to make patterns of the dresses. She then bought fabric and made dresses that looked just liked the ones in the catalog. I was often complemented on my clothes. Lillie sewed so well, she was paid to sew clothes for neighbors and friends.

Arterway and Lillie were a good-looking couple, who loved life and had a great sense of humor. They were married on March 14, 1917. They had nine children. I am the middle child. I was born on Mother's Day, May 11, 1924, on a small farm in Edgecomb County, North Carolina.

I called my parents "Daddy" and "Ma." They were honest, hard working people, who tried to instill these same virtues in their children. They stressed good manners, doing your best, having high self esteem, and respecting yourself and others. A verse they frequently recited to reinforce these qualities went like this:

Drive a nail right.
Hit it on the head.
Strike it with your might
While the iron is red.

All that you do,
Do it with your might.
Things done by halves
Are never done right.

In addition to virtues, they stressed doing well in school. My siblings and I were repeatedly told that good grades are not simply given but are "earned." They followed up by checking our school work every day. When my written assignments had errors, they reinforced the skills. I felt pressure to do well, but it was not unduly. And praise was given whenever it was deserved.

Harvest Time!
Me and neighboring children harvesting crops.
Photo from the author's collection.

•

chapter two

Sharecropping

Ma and Daddy worked as sharecroppers on farms throughout Eastern North Carolina. Sharecropping was a major business in the South after slavery was abolished in 1865. It was designed to give former slaves the opportunity to earn money for their labor which would support their families, and to provide former slave owners with the labor to work their farmlands. The sharecroppers lived on the farms and planted and harvested the crops. The farm owners and sharecroppers were to share equally in the profits of the harvest after the yearly expenses for operating the farm were deducted. However, most of the sharecroppers could not read or write. So some farm owners took advantage of them.

Throughout the year, the sharecroppers would charge to the country store food, clothing, and whatever else they needed to run the farm. After harvesting and selling the crops, sharecroppers who could not read or write had no idea of how much they owed the country store. The farm owners used this to their advantage by giving these sharecroppers money to pay on the debt to country stores. However, the amount of money was so small it never erased the debt which kept the sharecropper continually in debt to the farm owner and the country store. This unethical practice became a cycle repeated year after year, becoming a form of economical slavery because the sharecroppers were in financial bondage to the country stores. They could not move or look for new opportunities; they literally owed their souls to these stores.

But not Daddy! He kept a small notebook in the pocket of his work shirt. Whenever anything was charged to the country store, he wrote down the item, its cost, and purchase date. After the crops were harvested and sold, Daddy would pull out his notebook to insist that the yearly costs of operating the farm be deducted before the profits were divided. When some farm owners found they could not cheat him, they fired him. They decided Arterway Lane was "just too smart" and did not want him living on or working their land.

Sharecropping was a way of life for millions of people. It was the only way of life I knew. Most of the time we worked the farms with our bare hands. At other times, we used plows, tobacco trucks, and wagons drawn by horses and mules. During the winter season, Daddy threw wild oat seeds over all the fields to protect the topsoil from the severe cold weather. We began farming the land as soon as the winter weather departed, which was usually in March and worked until late October. In early Spring, the fields were plowed and disked, a process of smoothing the soil with spiked equipment. Bushes and large, wild patches of grass were cut from ditches to provide drainage during heavy rains. Then, the planting began.

The men reported to the fields at sunrise. They were responsible for plowing the ground. They mixed fertilizers and chemicals, called lime and crop soda, in the soil to increase the size and quality of the plants. First, they made rows, then they planted the seeds. Once the seeds sprouted up, they plowed the rows to remove grass and weeds.

The women and children joined the men in the fields by 7:00 a.m., bringing breakfast with them. When the plowing was completed, everyone worked together to rid the tobacco of worms, to shake peanuts, to harvest crops, and to "shock corn", which was a process of cutting and tying green corn stalks to poles to dry.

Shocking corn provided winter food for cows, horses, and mules.

Very few women plowed land. It was considered "men's work," and boys were trained to plow fields at an early age. Buddy was barely tall enough to hold the plow steady when he started plowing fields with Daddy. Following a stubborn mule, while carrying a plow up and down a field trying to make straight rows, could be a lonely job. But, the atmosphere in the fields was uplifting as labor was seasoned with storytelling, telling jokes, and hymn singing. On any given day choruses of "Swing Low Sweet Chariot," "When the Saints Go Marching In," and "Standing in the Need of Prayer" filled the air.

During the farming season only one family worked a farm unless they were considered "day workers" who were paid by the day. When we worked for daily wages the men were paid $.75 a day, the women $.50, and the children $.35.

Two or three families of day workers, often of different races, lived on a farm.

This was a startling contrast to life in the city. Back in the 1930s schools, restaurants, beaches, movie theaters, and even water fountains were separated according to race. Signs that read, "colored" or "whites only" were placed all over town to make sure everyone knew where they could or could not go. This was called segregation.

Once while laboring in the hot southern fields as day workers, the landowner paid a white man, called an overseer, to keep an eye on us. Occasionally he brought out a bucket of water to give us a drink. There was only one dried gourd, a long small stemmed dipper, to scoop the water out of the bucket. A white family was also "day working" the farm. They were given water first. Then, it was our turn to drink from the gourd. I remember hearing people whispering, "Wonder what he does with the gourd at the end of the day?" Nevertheless, the same gourd was in the bucket each time we were brought water.

At twelve noon, loud bells rang and a whistle in the nearest town blew. This was the signal for sharecroppers to go home, eat lunch, and rest for an hour before returning to the fields. Women and a few children were permitted to leave the fields early to give them time to get their wooden stoves hot and lunch ready.

While walking along the edge of the woods to return home, I often picked wild berries. Placing them in my hat, I saved them to eat on my way home in the evenings. Working in the fields could really work up an appetite. Fortunately, there was plenty of food.

My family usually ate meals together. After one of my parents blessed the food, a Bible verse was recited by each child and my other parent. Then, it was time to dig in. When the bells rang and whistle blew, letting us know it was time to return to the fields, I felt rested. I walked back to the fields and worked until sunset.

Sharecropping was unpopular with me. My attitude towards my work performance was poor; hence I used every imaginable scheme to get excused from field work. Sometimes I rubbed my nose until it started bleeding. Other times I purposely worked slower than anyone else. I often stopped working and propped one foot on the side of the hoe or complained of headaches. Daddy would look back at me and yell, "Somebody get over there and help Freda catch up!"

Since my parents kept telling me I had "hands of a teacher," I did not want to use my hands working in a scorching hot field. In the back of my mind a thought was dancing, "If you want to get off this farm, you better get a good education." My parents, who were not as naive as I thought, saw through my schemes. But, they too, believed I had a higher calling. So around 10:30 a.m. every morning they sent me home to begin cooking dinner.

I often wondered why Daddy and Ma decided to remain in Eastern North Carolina, where major crops such as cotton, corn, peanuts, peas, and tobacco were raised. By moving to an area where only cotton and tobacco were raised, there would have been less work for us to do!

As I grew older, it was almost impossible to get out of working

Thats me in the front, tying tobacco leaves for curing with my "hands of a teacher." Tobacco was the "money crop" and required more time than our other crops. *Photo from the author's collection.*

on the farm. I would cry on the last day of school. While some folks thought I was crying because I would miss my friends during summer break, the truth is, I was thinking about the hot summer sun. Visions of my caramel colored skin sweating and burning under the hot summer sun as I worked in the fields filled my mind. I just couldn't help from crying. To make matters worse, Daddy would tease me by saying, "Get out there in the sunshine and come back to your natural colors." This was his way of reminding me I would get a "suntan," since last year's suntan had worn off during the winter.

The seeds had already been planted during the Spring. So the first day of summer break was spent chopping weeds that would grow around the crops. This was done daily until the crops were large enough to protect themselves from weeds. When they reached this stage, the crops were considered "laid by," which meant they were permitted to grow on their own until harvest time. When the crops reached the "laid by" stage of their development, I was not as busy. But there was always work to be done.

Tobacco was referred to as the "money crop," because it consumed more time than any of the other crops. In early Spring, seeds were scattered in a small tobacco bed. Then the tobacco bed would be covered with a white net for protection from birds and wild animals. At the end of the school day, small boards were placed across the tobacco bed and grass was picked from among the plants. Logs were placed on each side of the tobacco bed to support the small boards that were used for seats while pulling the grass from the plants.

Growing tobacco was not only time consuming; it was difficult because tobacco plants, like temperamental people, must be handled with care. When the tobacco plants were large enough they were transferred to a field and set by hand. When rain was scarce, each plant was watered by hand. As the plants grew, suckers, a shoot from the lower part of the stem of a plant which retards the growth, grew on them. I had to break the suckers and blossoms from the top of each plant. This proved to be a frightening task because the suckers and blossoms were infested with long green worms. When I broke the suckers the worms would lean their heads back and snap at me. Sometimes clothespins were used to remove the worms which were placed in tin cups. Eventually, Daddy would empty the tin cups into a large bucket, later getting rid of the worms.

Unlike most plants, tobacco ripens from the bottom up. As the green leaves turned yellow, men, boys, and a few women would break them and place them in a tobacco truck. Tobacco trucks were long with flat siding and drawn by horses and mules. Once placed on the trucks the tobacco leaves were driven from the field. The leaves were then gathered in small bundles at a bench and tied by placing them on a stick and using twine to tie the leaves down. The sticks were then hung in tobacco barns for curing. Someone was responsible for watching the barn and checking the barn temperature night and day. Once cured the tobacco was removed from sticks and graded, which involved separating leaves according to similar colors and sizes. Then, the tobacco was tied in small bundles, placed on sticks without thread, and packed down until it was ready to take to the market. To keep tobacco soft and fresh, it was sprinkled with water, piled on the barn floor, and covered with wide sheets made from fertilizer bags.

Although I purposely performed poorly in most field work, I excelled in picking cotton. Daddy and Ma sparked my interest in picking cotton by starting a contest. They would pair the children according to their ages. The person from each pair who picked the most cotton would receive a nickel. I often won the cotton picking contest. After the cotton was picked it was stored in sheets and taken to a cotton gin to form into bales until it was ready for sale.

After the cotton crops were "laid by," they became infested with hard, grayish bugs called "boll weevils." I remember picking out the bugs and leaving them for Daddy to kill. When I was too small to pull a cotton sack, I would just pick the cotton and place it on the ground for one of my older siblings to pick up.

We often ate dinner in the cotton fields when the weather was cooler. Baked sweet potatoes, canned salmon, canned mackerel or home smoked meat, and bread were often served for dinner, along with water or soft drinks.

I dreaded harvesting peanuts because it was backbreaking labor. Growing on the bottom of plants, peanut plants were plowed up and each plant was shaken until the dirt fell off the peanuts. Tall poles with small slats attached to the bottom were placed in the field. After shaking, peanut vines were placed on the poles to make a stack. Nuts were placed toward the inner pole with vines covering them for protection from birds and wild animals. My back would feel as if it were breaking due to continually bending and shaking hundreds of peanuts.

When the peanuts dried, the men and boys hauled them to a machine operated by mules or horses. There the peanuts were separated and stored in bags for selling. Vines were formed into bales to be used as food for cows, horses, and mules. Some peanuts were reserved for feeding animals.

Working in corn fields caused me more physical pain than any other crop. The leaves were long, thin, and sharp. Moreover, the plants made my skin itch. I sustained many scrapes from corn stalks. However, the good uses made from corn far surpassed the physical inconveniences. Dried ears of corn were gathered by hand to use for food for the pigs, chickens, cows, horses and mules. Stalks were fed to cows. Grits and corn meal were also made from dried corn. Some grits were ground at home. Corn meal was processed at meal factories.

Growing and harvesting peas required little labor. They were thrown in rows and left pretty much alone until we picked them during the summer. In early Fall after the pods dried, the peas were picked, placed in feed bags, and whipped with a stick to separate the peas from the pods. On windy days buckets were filled with dried peas and pods and thrown in the air, letting the wind separate them. The peas would fall on a sheet made of fertilizer bags. They were then placed in bags to be used for family meals and as additional food for pigs, horses, and mules.

When I had free time, I was somewhat of a loner. I would take Ma's scissors, thread, needle, and old rags to the field, where I would spend hours alone making and dressing grass dolls. I also enjoyed reading my parents' old books. When I was nine-years-old I read *The Sinking of the Titanic* all by myself.

Sometimes I think my siblings wondered if my head were on right, since I walked in my sleep and exhibited such laziness while working in the field. However, it did not matter to me. I was too busy visualizing myself becoming a teacher like my favorite teacher, Mrs. Eason.

Sharecropping was exhausting work but I really enjoyed living on a farm. The countryside was my playground, the farm animals were my pets, and there were plenty of gardens and orchards.

Taking a break with my younger sister. (Left to right): Me and Lillian.
Photo from the author's collection

•

chapter three

Life on the Farm

L ife on the farm during the 1920s - 1940s was filled with excitement and hard work. I depended on family members for physical, mental, and moral support. Although I had few material belongings, there was plenty of food and clothing.

The farm houses we lived in were built on a brick foundation and stood about a foot in the air to allow for cleaning and to eliminate snakes. I found most of the houses unattractive because they were not painted on the outside and did not have plaster on the walls. Usually, the walls were simply boards of plywood nailed to the frame.

There were usually two bedrooms, which had enough room for two double beds. Beds were also placed in the living room and kitchen to provide enough sleeping space for my large family. The kitchens were often large and had wood stoves and cabinets, a table, and chairs. Red brick fireplaces were in the bedrooms and living rooms. A few of the houses had porches, but most of them just had concrete or board steps below the front door.

Holes would form in the plywood board ceilings enabling me to watch the moon and stars at night. On rainy nights water would fall into my bedroom from the boards and the leaky roof. The bed would be moved to avoid getting soaked by the rainfall.

When rain continued to fall on the bed, a pan or a small tub was placed under the drips. In the wintertime flour paste was used to put wall paper on the walls. I would fill the holes with rags or cotton and paste beautiful pictures from magazines on the walls around the beds. However, I was not permitted to paste paper on the walls near the fireplace because the papers would be too close to the fireside.

During the summer months, beds were infested with small, round, brownish bugs called bed bugs. Contrary to some people's beliefs, bed bugs were not due to uncleanness. Wherever they came from, it was a relief when they disappeared during the winter months. In the summertime I would pick them from the beds. Then the beds, slats, and springs were washed in very hot water and the mattresses were put out in the hot sunshine. I slept on palates on the floor most of the summer. Bedbugs were not as bad on the floor. But they returned during summers.

Mattresses for my bed were usually made from soft, dried corn shucks, which were pulled from dried ears of corn, or from dried grass. Ma made the mattress covers. When the mattresses were filled they became very tall. After sleeping on them for a few weeks they were pressed down to a normal size. I enjoyed sleeping on them. Whenever we had company I tried to avoid touching the beds because dried corn shucks and dried grass certainly would rattle!

As for the farm animals, we raised our own pigs. In the spring they were penned in an area. As the land was needed for farming, they were closed in the pig pen. Pigs required regular feedings of slop, corn, weeds, watermelons, and other vegetables. I was embarrassed to feed them on Sunday afternoons because we usually had company. I would pull a few weeds, give them a little corn, pour a little slop, and quickly return to the house. About two hours later the pigs would squeal, as if they had nothing to eat. Daddy would politely say, "The pigs are still hungry. Go and feed them." Despite my embarrassment, I could not say, "no," to Daddy. So off I went to feed the pigs again.

Lillian, my younger sister, and me.
Photo from the author's collection

When the weather began to get cold, it was "hog killing time." Daddy would ask men from adjoining farms to assist with this gruesome task. Large tin cans were filled with water from the pump and heated over an open fire. A rifle was used to shoot each pig which afterwards was dipped in hot water, scalded, and pulled out to scrape the hair off. After removing the hair, each pig was hung on a pole by its feet and cut open to remove the heart, kidneys, and intestines.

Then the intestines, which were called "chitterlings," were taken to a field, cleaned, and washed immaculately at the outdoor pump. They were then cooked outdoors over an open fire in a black iron pot. While cooking the chitterlings smelled awful! The strong odor was more than my nose could bear. Although chitterlings smelled bad, they tasted so good! When the chitterlings were ready, I put a little vinegar on mine to season them. Then I ate as many as Ma put on my plate.

Daddy and his helpers would cut the hogs into hams, shoulders, pork chops, pork roasts, and side meat. Hearts, livers, and other internal organs were used for meals soon after the pigs were killed or combined with pig ears and feet to make a dish called "souse." Souse meat would jell due to its consistency of pig feet and ears. After it chilled, it was cut in small squares and placed in jars of vinegar. Souse was served with dinner or as a snack.

Leftover meats from trimming the pork was used for making sausage. The sausage was stuffed in raw, small intestines. All the meats were salted, smoked by wood, and placed in smokehouses for storage. Fat from the hogs was used to make lard and cracklings. Some skin was roasted. So many dishes were made from "hog killings," there was a saying, "Everything is saved from the pig but its grunt." I was always sad during hog killing time because I had become friendly with a few of the pigs. I cried when my favorites met their fate.

Chickens were plentiful on our farm, so we rarely bought eggs. Like the pigs, the chickens' fate was to become dinner. Before killing them, they were shut up in a box and fed corn to "clean them out." Buddy usually killed a chicken by taking it by the head and slinging it around in the air until the head flew off. Sometimes he would place the neck on a piece of wood, chopping the head off. The headless chicken would then jump wildly around in the yard until it died. It seemed rather cruel killing animals. Nevertheless, this thought was dismissed from my mind as soon as the chicken was prepared and placed on the table!

Our pets included dogs, chickens and other animals. Three dogs that were special to me were: Spot, Snowball, and Ranger. Spot was white with brown spots. Snowball was small with fluffy white fur, and Ranger had large brown and white spots and long fur. Ranger was a friendly dog, but he was very inactive because he slept a lot. Spot was my pal, always following me as I picked wild berries for dessert. He could sense the presence of a snake or wild animal and would growl loudly to warn me of danger. Snowball was Daddy's hunting dog. Daddy told me that one day he was tip toeing on dry leaves to sneak up on a wild animal, when he looked back he saw Snowball tip toeing, too!

Pip was our pet chicken. She hatched too late in the Fall to survive living outside in the cold chicken house. Therefore, we kept her in the house during the winter. When she was a chick, I put her in a box at night and laid it in my bed. As soon as Spring arrived, she went outside. In the evenings she would walk down the road to meet me as I came home from school. She never related very well to the barnyard chickens. One day Pip saw her reflection in a bucket of water. Thinking it was another chicken, she jumped in the bucket and drowned. We had a children's "play" funeral and buried Pip. In addition to dogs and a chicken, there were many cats and kittens.

Doing things the right way often caused me to be drafted to do extra work. Some of my assignments would have been given to my siblings if I performed them in the sloppy manner I reserved for field work. Daddy and Ma would often say, "Let Freda do it." This

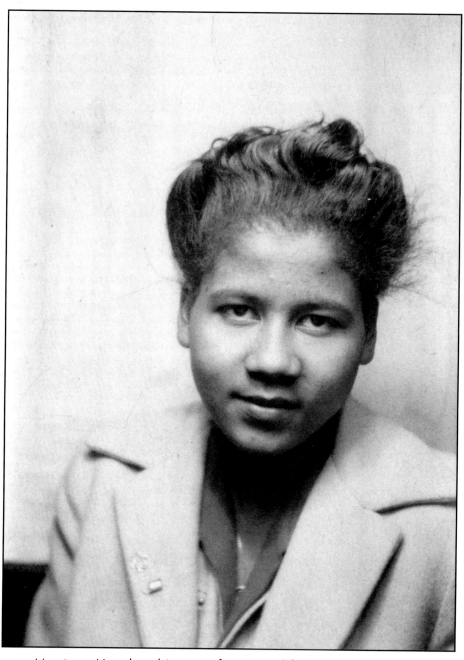

My sister, Hazel and I were often paired for household chores.
Photo from the author's collection.

My brothers, Buddy and Linwood.
Photo from the author's collection.

was their way of recognizing my willingness to follow directions.

Hazel and I, who were closest in age, were often paired for household chores. For some reason, we could never get together to do a job as we should. When Daddy and Ma went to town we were asked to scrub floors. I would sweep and scrub half of the floor while Hazel played. Then Hazel would come in and sweep and scrub the other half while I played.

Most of the children assisted with washing clothes. The white and dark clothes were separated and put into iron pots over an outdoor fire to boil. Then they were washed in a tub using a scrub board to remove the dirt. After a clear water rinse and a bluing rinse, some clothes were starched. They were all hung outside to dry. Ironing was performed with a flat iron, which was heated on a wood stove or in front of the open fireplace. Irons were cleaned by wiping them on old rags, then on brown paper bags to make sure they would not scorch the clothes. I tried to avoid scorching my clothes because I did not want to re-wash a scorched garment. I could just hear Ma and Daddy saying, "Things done by halves are never done right."

Although Ma made most of my clothes, getting something new and "store bought" was a real treat. On these occasions Daddy would take a few of us to town and leave the rest with Ma. Daddy shopped for coats, shoes, socks, and sweaters.

Shoes were priced from $.59 to $.99. Other items were also cheap back in the 1930s.

Trying on clothes and shoes was exciting. If I tried on something that I did not particularly like and Daddy felt that it was what he could afford, he would say, "I like what you have on. When you are wearing something other people are going to be looking at you. Pick something that other people like sometimes, even if you do not like it yourself."

While in town Daddy treated us to ice cream, hot dogs, and sodas. This was in the 1930s and segregation was in full force. We were served through a window, and entered stores and restaurants through side doors. After being served we had to go outside to eat. The benches that lined the streets, the public water fountains, and the rest rooms were all segregated. Although everything was supposed to be "separate but equal," the places that had signs marked "colored" were run down compared to the ones with signs marked "white." Nevertheless, everyone spoke kindly to me and I considered our trips to town eventful experiences.

Two things Daddy did not shop for during our trips to town were fruits and vegetables. Preserving and canning fruits and vegetables eliminated the need to purchase these items from the country store, which reduced our winter grocery bills. As soon as crops were "laid by," we began canning and drying. Whenever I complained about gathering and preparing them, Daddy and Ma would say, "You complain now, but we'll see how much you complain when it's cold and there's warm food on the table."

While working in the gardens and orchards there was a delightful, yet competitive atmosphere amongst neighbors. Frequently farm families compared the number of jars canned. It was not unusual to hear someone boasting of canning two or three hundred jars.

Canning was a chief priority. Jars were bought, picked up from the roadside or saved from previous years. Apples, peaches, and pears were gathered and hauled to the water pump for rinsing. After rinsing, they were placed in a tub of water. I peeled and cut fruit until my "hands of a teacher" grew sore. Water and sugar were placed in a large, tin cooking container on a wood stove. When I finished peeling, fruit was added and left to cook.

Before canning, jars were washed and placed in a large containers to boil for sterilization. The cooked fruit was placed in each jar and an elastic rubber band was rolled near the top of each jar. Then the top was closed loosely and left to cool. After cooling, the caps were tightened and the jars were stored away.

Although I complained about canning and preserving fruit from our orchard, it didn't stop me from sneaking into our neighbors' orchard. Mr. and Mrs. Draughn, an elderly couple who lived

43

across the road from us, had the prettiest fruit imaginable. While Mr. Draughn was out farming, his wife, who could barely walk, would sit on the porch. One of my sibling would spy to see where she was sitting, while I would steal fruit from trees that Mrs. Draughn could not see.

One day while we were in the backyard sneaking plums, Mrs. Draughn overheard us. When I saw her hobbling around the house heading in our direction, I ran into the outdoor toilet to hide. I was so scared. Fortunately, she didn't look in the outdoor toilet. Sometimes I was sure Mr. and Mrs. Draughn knew I was stealing fruit from their orchard, but I don't think that they ever told Ma and Daddy. Relieved, I would volunteer to help them with chores such as carrying water or fire wood inside their home.

Like the Draughn's juicy plums, grapes ripened during the summer hurricane season. I enjoyed eating them; however, too many grapes fell to the ground during the strong winds. Daddy and Ma instructed us to save the grape hulls for preserving. Daddy also used the grapes to make wine. Daddy would place the grapes in a tin tub. Then I washed my feet and got in the tub and crushed the grapes for wine making. It was fun standing there with grape juice oozing from my toes.

I loved grapes, particularly the grape preserves Ma made. But, since grape preserves turned black, I was ashamed to take grape jelly biscuits in my lunch box because the jelly made my biscuits look dirty. But I never threw them away; they tasted too good!

Sometimes I could not wait to eat the fruit that grew in the orchards. Eating fruit before it was fully ripe caused my teeth to ache whenever I ate warm food. This condition was called "teeth on edge." However, this did not hinder me! Food was plentiful on the farm, especially during the summer when so many fresh fruit and vegetables were ripe.

Canning vegetables was an unpleasant chore. Frequently neighbors would give us tomatoes to can. The tomatoes were placed in a bag which I carried over my shoulders. Sticky, red, tomato juice would run from the ripe tomatoes and soil my back, adding to the discomfort caused by the hot sun. Tomatoes were canned alone or mixed with corn and lima beans for making soup. Corn, okra, and string beans were also amongst the vegetables I canned.

Making preserves and pickles required more attention than canning. Preserves were made by cooking whole or large pieces of fruit or tomatoes in a little water with enough sugar to make them very sweet. Sometimes spices were added. The cooking time seemed long, as the preserves jelled over medium heat. We stirred frequently until the preserves completely jelled. Then we placed them in sterilized jars as we did with all canned goods.

Pickles were made from cucumbers, peaches, and watermelon rinds. After soaking a few days in salt and water, they were removed and washed enough to remove excess salt. They were placed in a container with sugar, spices, water, vinegar, and cooked slowly until done.

Drying fruits started early because the fruit did not need to be fully ripe. The wind would blow, causing the fruit to fall to the ground. Some of the fruit was fed to pigs while others were peeled, cut up, and placed on an old sheet. The fruit was then placed on top of a barn during the day permitting the sun to draw up the juice until they were dry. Dried fruit was stored in bags and hung on the kitchen walls for use as needed.

We did not work on Saturdays. I spent some weekends helping Ma. I would walk with her to missionary meetings, fish with her on the river banks, dig worms to bait her hooks, and get up on Sunday mornings to help her fix breakfast.

I spent time with Daddy, too.

Daddy and I would go fishing together, but I always got nervous when he extended his fishing pole to help me walk across a log extending over a canal. I sat at the tobacco barn with Daddy at times when he was curing tobacco. I would see foxes coming out of the woods but I was not afraid of foxes. Daddy always had a dog with him who would chase the foxes away. However, I was most thankful for Daddy's gun which he kept loaded nearby.

Daddy permitted me to clean hunted animals. This was a meticulous undertaking because furs had to be removed without making unnecessary holes in them. Then the furs were tacked on boards to dry and mailed to a catalog company. They were then used to make fur garments. When I finished cleaning wild animals, I had no appetite for eating them. I have cleaned fox, squirrels, muskrats, mink, coons, rabbits, and opossums.

Hazel, Buddy, and I developed a passion for rambling through fields and woods when the farm work was finished. We often picked wild grapes and gathered hickory nuts and walnuts. Buddy had boxes that were used to trap rabbits. Hazel and I would walk with him to check the boxes to see if he caught any rabbits. When he missed catching a rabbit in a particular box for a short time, he would give the box to Hazel or me. As soon as we caught a rabbit in the box, to our dismay he would reclaim it.

One day while digging around a stump in the woods, we found an opossum and three baby opossums. Excited about our discovery, we took them all home and put them in a box. One rainy night they mysteriously disappeared. Daddy explained their disappearance by saying that opossums disappear when it rains. But I figured, he probably let them out, because they were wild animals and it was dangerous for us to play with them.

Growing up on the farm was so much fun. But all the fun could not erase the seriousness of the "hands of a teacher" prophecy my parents had ingrained in my soul. Sometimes I thought the farm work would take its toll on my teacher looking hands. However it was my childhood accidents that proved to do the most damage.

●

chapter four

Accidents Will Happen

Was I accident prone? Or was it just my imagination? I probably suffered the most injuries of all my sisters and brothers. Most of the accidents were beyond my control. But a few were the inescapable consequences of disobeying parental rules.

Whatever the cause of the accidents the results were usually the same, painful embarrassment and lying to cover up the obvious truth.

Many of my accidents involved farm animals, such as cows, pigs, and calves.

Buddy and I shared the responsibility of caring for the cows. We fed them, gave them water, took them to the field to graze, and returned them to their stalls.

Taking the cows out to graze was challenging. We led them with a chain attached around the necks, found a grassy area, secured the chains to a long stake, and knocked it deep in the ground. Sometimes a cow would walk round and round the stake while eating causing the chain to become too short for grazing. When this happened, we would go over to the stake and unwrap the chains.

One day while Buddy was knocking a stake in the ground a cow looked at me, blew dust from the ground, and charged toward me. I was so frightened. But before I could run, Buddy hit the stake just in time to jerk the cow backwards, preventing an attack. Despite this incident, the cow did not appear ferocious so I continued to assist with its care.

Cows, like chickens, seem to panic during thunderstorms. Daddy had warned me to avoid letting cows run loose because he feared they would trample our crops. Running through the corn field was dangerous to cows because the sharp leaves on the corn would cut and damage the cow's milk bag. So whenever a storm was approaching, I would take the cows to the barn.

One stormy day, while Buddy was helping Daddy in the field, I walked over to a grazing cow to remove its chain and return it to the barn. As I removed the chain from the stake, there was a loud clash of thunder. Immediately, the cow started running through the orchard. I held the chain firmly and was dragged around tree trunks. When my hands began to bleed, I became frightened and released the chain. I did not want my "hands of a teacher" to become torn leaving ugly scars. The cow ran straight into the cornfield knocking down cornstalks in its path.

Daddy, Buddy, and the other children were coming from the field to avoid the storm when the sounds of my screams reached them. They looked around and saw me lying on the ground and the cow running wildly through the corn field. After checking to make sure I was not injured, everyone ran to the corn field to try to catch the cow. Daddy knew that I had tried hard to restrain the cow when he saw my bloody hands, so I did not get a scolding. But, I still felt a little embarrassed.

Calves are usually frisky and playful. I would oblige our calf by freeing her to run and jump in the fields. Since calves are much smaller than a grown cow, it's easier to manipulate the chain to restrain them. I would always take the calf to the outdoor pump to get water before taking her to graze. Since there was no central water system on the farm, tubs and tin drums were placed near the outdoor pump to catch rain water for the farm animals.

One day after drinking from the tin drums, the calf jerked as if frightened. I fell flat on my back. The calf ran a short distance, then stopped. She then turned around and looked at me lying helpless on the ground. I got up feeling dizzy. My head felt as if it had popped. I walked over to the calf, took her to the grazing area, knocked the stake in the ground, attached the chain and left her to graze.

Another cow accident involves my vain attempt to milk a cow. I would often accompany my older sister, Lillie, as she milked the cow early in the mornings. Before milking the cow, its foot was raised and tied to a stake to prevent the cow from walking during the milking process. The cow's tail was also tied down to prevent it from smacking Lillie in the face. As soon as Lillie finished, the tail was untied.

One day I decided to see if I could milk the cow, too. As I reached for the cow's milk bag, its tail slapped me right across my face, leaving long red marks. When I went to school, my class-mates asked me about the marks. "Oh, uh, I-I-I fell. I fell on my face," I stuttered, trying to conceal that truth that was written all over my face.

The pigs were another story. During the early Fall pigs were fed sweet potato vines, which grew very long and were filled with leaves. We would cut the vines and take them to the pigpen. As we drew near, the pigs would rush to the sides of the pen and lean on them. Since there were many pigs, someone had to get in the pen and chase them back. "I will shoo them away," I told Ma, while climbing the fence. I jumped into the pigpen and started chasing the pigs. Then suddenly, I tripped over on a corn cob. "I broke my arm, I broke my arm!" I cried.

Ma threw the vines in the pig pen and reached over the fence to examine my bent arm. She grabbed my bent arm tenderly, straight-ened it, and along with my siblings pulled me from the pen. We walked to the house where my wrist was placed in a wash pan filled with warm water. Ma then added turpentine and she sat beside me, gently rubbing my wrist until Daddy came home from hunting.

As soon as Daddy found out my arm was broken, he immediately walked outside to break off a fresh tree limb that he could use to twiddle splints. He placed the splints around my arm to keep the broken bone in place and put a bandage around the wound. There was no phone to call a doctor.

That night I slept in the bed with Ma. Throughout the night she often awoke me to ask me if I had any pains. The wrist hurt a little and I felt scared, but I always answered, "No."

The next morning Daddy got up very early to take tobacco to the market in Tarboro. He loaded the wagon, leaving room for the three of us, Daddy, Ma, and me, to sit. After breakfast we got on the wagon to begin our five mile journey to Tarboro. Daddy was taking me to see the doctor and taking the tobacco to the market.

After unloading the tobacco Daddy was excused to take me to the doctor's office. The mules and wagon were left in an area reserved for them until we were ready to return home.

As we walked the short distance to the doctor's office, I felt very nervous. I still remembered my first visit to the doctor to remove an infected sore on my neck. That doctor did not use anesthesia and it hurt! This doctor talked quietly to me as he removed the bandage and splints. He pressed my left wrist and asked me if I felt any pain. It hurt! But I continued to answer, "No."

The doctor told my parents that my wrist was broken, and that he would straighten it and place it in a iron cast. He mixed plaster of paris in water and placed my wrist in the cast, leaving my fingers free. Plaster of paris was applied to the arm and around the cast. A thick white bandage covered everything. A sling was placed around my neck to prevent the arm from swinging. The doctor asked Daddy and Ma to bring me back in four weeks to have the cast removed. We left the doctor's office and returned to the tobacco market. After the tobacco was sold, Daddy bought cookies and cheese to eat on our trip home.

My parents decided that I would not be allowed to attend school with a broken wrist. I dreaded missing school. When Mrs.

Olive Eason, my fourth grade teacher, learned I could not attend school due to a broken wrist, she sent a note home by Buddy. The note stated that she would like me to return to school, and that she would supervise me in order to eliminate further injury to my arm. Ma and Daddy agreed.

When I returned to school some children ran from me because they had never seen anyone wearing an iron cast. The teachers explained the purpose of the cast, to calm their fears. The four weeks went by quickly and soon it was time to have the cast removed. My arm felt a bit useless due to inactivity. But the important thing was: it was healed!

Curious, strong-willed, and somewhat of a loner, I was determined to express my independence. Rather than listening to my parents, I wanted to make my own judgments. Whenever I was told not to do something, I would try to find out why it was forbidden by doing it. This defiant attitude often got me in trouble, leaving scars to prove it.

Once I jumped out of a tree that had a rusty nail extending from its bark. The nail left a long scar on my left thumb. Unfortunately, my wound did not get me excused from washing dishes!

One summer I was warned not to play on a swing that hung from a tree in the wooded area near our house. Unable to resist the temptation, I decided to go to swing alone. I hopped on and began swinging, happily, until a piece of wire from the chain stuck under one of my fingernails, causing that fingernail to never grow properly again.

I was not permitted to look under a hen setting on eggs, which would cause the hen to crack the eggs before they were hatched. Once I took an ax to chop a stick to raise the hen so I could see if eggs were hatching. As I was chopping, a piece of wood flew through my upper lip leaving a small hole which began to bleed badly. Lying to Ma, I ran in the house crying, "I tried to cut wood to start a fire in the kitchen stove."

My favorite elementary school teacher, Mrs. Olive Eason, in 1937.
She taught me from fourth through seventh grades and allowed
me to substitute as a teacher when other teachers were absent.
Photo from the author's collection.

After inspecting my lip, she asked someone to bring her the bottle of horse medicine, which back then was used for people and animals. "I don't want that horse medicine on my mouth!" I yelled. Despite my protest, Ma smoothed the horse medicine on my lip. And it worked! The wound healed nicely. But I still have a scar on my upper lip, a constant reminder of the times when medicines for farm animals were used on people.

Yet, taking horse medicine did not deter me from disobedience. The dirt roads where we lived were covered with pine tar. While walking to and from school, I would pick up pieces of tar and chew it. Somehow, I got a piece of tar stuck at the root of a plait on the back of my head. I pulled and pulled, but could not get it out. When I got home I took a pair of scissors and cut the tar out. While combing my hair, Ma discovered that a chunk was missing. This time, I told her the truth. Although I did not get a whipping, I was told not to chew anymore tar. But that did not stop me. I still chewed tar, but I avoided putting it close to my head.

One of my fifth grade classmates, a girl named Vertella, owned an expensive ring. It only cost 10 cents, but in the 1930s 10 cents was a lot of money for a child. Because everyone admired it and no one else had one, she decided to let each girl in our classroom wear the ring for a week. When it was my turn to wear the ring, it would not fit over my fat knuckles. So I took the ring home and forced it on by dipping my hand in warm soapy water.

When it was time to give the ring to the next girl in class, there was no warm water to help me get it off. I pulled and pulled but the ring wouldn't budge. During recess, a classmate pumped cold water over my hand. By now, my finger was swelling and turning blue. Fortunately, someone went into the school building and called my teacher.

Mrs. Eason walked out, looked at my hand and said, "The ring must come off before blood poison sets in." Then she ran back into the building, got some string, attached it to the two sides of the ring and started pulling and tugging it. All the children on the playground gathered around us to see what was going on. My siblings stood with me, as Mrs. Eason pulled and tugged. Finally after one hard yank, off came the ring. And my skin! Blood trickled down my finger as the ring was removed. My ring finger still has the battle scars of my experience. Never did I wear another ring until I purchased a high school class ring at 16.

Another hand injury occurred one rainy day while I was standing on the front porch lighting firecrackers and throwing them on the lawn. After lighting a firecracker, it fell on the porch. Although Daddy had warned us about picking up firecrackers when they failed to explode, the porch was wet and I thought that it was safe because the light stem looked like it had burned out. As soon as I picked up the firecracker, it exploded in my hand blowing off part of my fingernail and leaving a huge blood blister on my right pointer. The excessively blown skin never grew back to its normal size. The accident happened so fast I was baffled. Seeing we could not afford a doctor, Daddy applied a home remedy until the hand healed.

It seemed awkward that many of my accidents left scars on my hands and nails. Since my hands were destined to become "hands of a teacher," I knew I would have to stay out of trouble. But that's easier said than done when you're a kid. As the weather grew cooler I stayed in the house more, spending time with my family around the fireside. So some of the temptations went away.

Achievement and Effort

Subjects	*A	*E	A	E	A	E	A	E	Term	A	E	A	E	A	E	A	E	Term
Reading	a	a	a	a						a	a	a	a					
Language	a	a	a	a						a	a	a	a					
Writing	a	a	a	a						a	a	a	a					
Spelling	a	a	a	a						a	a	a	a					
Arithmetic	a	a	a	a						a	a	a	a					
Geography	a	a	a	a						a	a	a	a					
N. C. History																		
U. S. History																		
European Hist.	a	a	a	a						a	a	a	a					
Citizenship																		
Health	a	a	a	a						a	a	a	a					
Physical Ed.																		
Science																		
Music	a	a	a	a						a	a	a	a					
Art																		
Days Absent	3	2	4															
Times Tardy																		

Promoted to Grade 7

*A=ACHIEVEMENT
A—93-100
B—85- 92
C—77- 84
D—70- 76
E—Failure

*E=EFFORT
A—Superior effort
B—Ordinary effort
C—Deficient effort
Cooperation of parents is sought in explaining or eliminating effort marks of C.

Parents are requested to sign and return this report and to confer with principal or teachers when progress does not appear satisfactory.

Parent's Signature:

A. W. Lane.
Lillie Lane.
B. W. Lane.

A. W. Lane
A. W. Lane
A. W. Lane
A. W. Lane

O. S. Eason _____, Teacher

My sixth grade report card, signed by Ma, Daddy, and Mrs. Eason.
Ma and Daddy signed report cards around the fireside.

•

chapter five

Around the Fireside

The weather grew cooler and the days grew shorter from October to April. During these months the fireplaces in our home took on special significance.

The practical use of the fireplace was to serve as a heating system. As a result there were fireplaces in each room, except the kitchen where there was a large wood stove.

Back then fireplaces were not designed to conserve heat. Since most of the heat went up the chimney, it was necessary to sit very close to the fireplace to get warm. My legs would develop blisters from overexposure to the heat. The blisters would burst and leave permanent scars, which were called "fire blossoms". To prevent my legs from developing blisters and fire blossoms, Ma and Daddy insisted that I always cover my legs with old quilts or some other heavy covering to protect them.

To conserve wood during the daytime, only the fireplace in the largest bedroom was lit. Whenever company came over, a fire was started in the fireplace in the living room. Occasionally, Daddy and Ma would light the fireplace in their bedroom.

Despite the threat of blisters and fire blossoms, sitting around the fireplace with my family was a special time. It provided an opportunity for me to ask Ma and Daddy questions about "old sayings" I heard and common practices that I observed.

I often wondered why people would turn around and go back home if a black cat crossed their path or place a horseshoe over their front doors to keep evil out. I would hear folks saying "If tears come down your eyes while peeling an onion, go stick your head in a chicken house," and "When it rains and the sun is shining, the devil is beating his wife." I never understood why people said and believed these things, but one of my favorite sayings was "Every tub stands on its own bottom."

Sometimes while sitting around the fireplace, my sisters and I helped Ma with quilting. Ma usually made bed coverings of two layers of cloth filled with wool, cotton, or feathers and held in place by stitching the designs by hand. While not working on the farm during the summer, Ma would cut patterns for quilt squares. I would take the patterns, cut the squares, and sew them using scraps left from Ma's sewing. Squares were sewed together to make the top of the quilt and the bottom was made from a wide sheet of cloth. During cold weather ladies who lived close to each other would help one another quilt. I helped on weekends by threading needles, holding lamps to help them see better, and doing a little hand stitching.

The unfinished quilt was placed on two poles and rolled, leaving enough unrolled sections for the ladies to sit around and quilt. As a section was finished more would be unrolled until it was all finished. The poles holding the quilting were placed on chairs and raised to a comfortable level to accommodate the women. Homemade quilts were very attractive with their one-of-a-kind designs. Squares were made from cotton prints of flowers, dots, and geometric designs. Usually measuring about six feet, three inches, quilts were heavy after they were filled with cotton. Dyes with fragrant aromas were used to color the cotton fabrics. I enjoyed smelling the floral scents of the new quilts while snuggling up under them at night

In addition to quilting and talking, we also did homework near the fireside.

With no electricity, oil lamps were placed on round tables near the fireplace. Daddy and Ma always sat through our homework assignments and assisted whenever needed. The older siblings would also assist the younger ones.

Because Buddy missed school a lot from having to help Daddy with the jobs that were reserved for men and boys, he and I were in the same grade. I assumed the responsibility of trying to teach him what he missed in school due to absenteeism.

We had reading assignments every night. As we progressed to higher grades, we were given assignments in language, geography, history, health, spelling, and handwriting. We did not study science in elementary school. Music was confined to singing. Music books were not available for children. Therefore, lyrics were learned by memory or by repeating words after the teacher. Later, when I looked in a songbook, I discovered that I had substituted words that sounded like the words I thought I heard.

We frequently ate and cooked around the fireside. When we arrived from school Ma would have dinner cooking. Collard greens, rutabagas, turnips, or cabbage were cooked in a black iron pot with smoked meat, ham, or side meat which was the main meat for dinner. An iron frying pan was placed on coals to fry chicken, fish, steak, or any other meat requiring frying. Sweet potatoes were boiled in an iron tea kettle. Corn bread was cooked in an iron bread pan and flipped over when one side was done. Canned vegetables and other foods were warmed or cooked in black iron utensils.

When it snowed, I would catch birds and cook them over the fireside. I trapped them by using a wooden hand board that was used for scrubbing clothes. After propping the washing boards up with a stick and placing bread crumbs under the board, I tied a long string to the stick. Then I ran the string through a window where I waited for birds to come under the wash boards to eat the crumbs.

As soon as a bird walked under the board, I would pull the string and watch the board fall smothering it. The bird was picked of its feathers and cut down the back. The insides were removed; then the bird was washed. Afterwards, I would place the bird on a long piece of wire and hold it over the fireside, watching it while it was roasting.

We also roasted peanuts and potatoes in hot ashes. Popcorn was roasted in an iron pan. Hickory nuts, pecans, and walnuts were cracked by hand or with the assistance of a hammer and brick as we prepared them for eating.

After all fireside activities were completed, it was time for folktales. There were no children's books; therefore, Daddy made up the tales. Some of them were so frightening I was afraid to go to sleep, especially since we slept in the dark to preserve oil.

One tale I remember fondly was about "Dem Bones." Daddy would say, "While sitting by the fire dem foot bones jumped on the coals and began to dance. Then dem ankle bones joined dem foot bones and danced. Next came dem leg bones, dem thigh bones, back bones, breast bones, arm bones, neck bone, and head bone. After dancing on the hot coals, dem bones came out of the fireplace and danced around all who sat by the fire. Then, dem bones started to disappear in the same order as they appeared." I would often imagine that head bone dancing alone in the air!

When it was time for bed I was so nervous. I knew that it was just a tale, but Daddy made it sound so realistic that I could visualize it. Finally, we said our prayers, said good night to our parents, and jumped into bed.

In the morning a fire was started in the bedroom fireplace. Since I often went skating on patches of winter ice in my high-top shoes, my shoes usually froze overnight. So I placed them near the fireside to thaw them. The winters seemed much colder in the 20s, 30s, and 40s than it is today. Even the drinking water in the bedroom would freeze after the fire went out.

I was not fond of getting up, washing up, and dressing in the cold. Lillie had the responsibility of getting the children up. And I gave her the biggest problem. When she called me I would pretend to be asleep. This would not stop Lillie. She would take the covers off me and I would get between the two mattresses. When she threatened to call Ma, I would quickly jump out of the bed.

Fully dressed for school, I ate breakfast in the kitchen. In winter I wore long underwear, full bloomers, three slips, a dress, sweater, black stockings, and high top-laced shoes. Buddy wore long underwear, pants, shirt, sweater, very heavy socks and high top shoes. We also wore heavy winter coats, hoods, and gloves. By the end of April the weather grew warmer and I began shedding the heavy winter clothes.

Checking report cards was a task my parents did around the fireside. Report cards were sent home eight times a year. My parents looked at all the report cards. Yet I never noticed them comparing them nor offering to pay us for making good grades. They probably felt each child was doing the best that could be expected, especially since they observed us doing homework exercises. Daddy usually lined us up from oldest to youngest and then signed each report card. My report card usually had straight A's; nevertheless, I never felt any different from my siblings due to my high grades.

I often wonder if the times that I spent around the fireside with Daddy and Ma helping my brothers and sisters with their lessons, fueled their desire to "make a teacher out of me." Perhaps it was doing these daily lessons that they noticed I had "hands like a teacher."

I always looked forward to Christmas season because my "hands like a teacher" would get a much needed rest during the two week Christmas vacation.

•

chapter six

Christmas Time

In the Fall the farm crops were mature enough to survive with the grass. Hence it was no longer necessary to chop grass, which left me with extra time on my hands. I spent most of my free time with Buddy and Hazel. We walked through the woods looking for small trees. When we spotted one we liked, we would bend it over and sit on it pretending we were riding a horse. Although our other siblings joined us at times, Buddy, Hazel, and I were usually a threesome.

As the days grew colder, thoughts of Christmas filled my mind. While walking through the woods with my siblings, I would look for a cedar tree to claim as our future Christmas tree. When we found the right tree, we would tie a long piece of cloth around the trunk. We advertised amongst our neighbors where our tree was located and described the marking tied around the tree trunk. This was our insurance that the neighbors would not cut it down. When Christmas drew near the tree was finally cut down and placed in the room where we sat by the fireside. Our Christmas trees were so tall they touched the ceiling.

The houses never had electricity; therefore, Christmas tree decorations consisted of store bought colorful bulbs, artificial snowflakes, strung popcorn, and ornaments made from construction paper. My siblings and I showed off our artistic creativity by drawing and cutting out Santa Claus, candlesticks, bells, stars, and angels to be hung on the tree. After decorating the tree, I would stand back and admire its beauty, as the fresh cedar scent of the newly cut tree filled the house.

Decorating trees in the 1920s, 30s and 40s seemed more exciting than today. There was complete family involvement in putting the tree up, decorating it, and storing the decorations for the next year. I often wondered how our neighbors might be decorating their trees because I was competitve and wanted to have the best Christmas tree. During visits from neighbors, there were discussions about the trees. Of course, I always felt our tree was the biggest, best decorated, and prettiest! I suspect that the same feeling existed in each home.

As for the rest of the house, red, yellow, and green streamers made out of construction paper were placed all around the tree, across the ceilings, around the doors and windows, and up and down the hallway. Part of the holly berry bushes were cut and placed on doors and windows, while others graced the fireplace mantle or were placed in jars and used as centerpieces for tables.

There was always extra special foods during the Christmas holiday. Daddy always bought a large round box of delicious sharp cheese. The cheese was round shaped like a pound cake, but slightly wider. Ma would make cheese and eggs, macaroni and cheese, cookies and cheese, and hot cheese biscuits.

Baking cakes and pies started about two days before Christmas. Empty metal lard cans were saved during the year to store baked goodies. At least two cakes and eight pies could be stored in each lard can.

We did not own a refrigerator, so I would sit out in the snow cooling chocolate icing until it was thick enough to spread on a cake. The first batch of baking usually included a chocolate cake, plain cake, coconut cake, and black walnut cake. Pies were made from coconuts and sweet potatoes. After all of the cakes and pies were eaten, a second batch was made. Due to cold weather, baked goods remained fresh stored in cans.

Barbecue pig was always served during the holidays. A barbecue pit was dug near one of the woodpiles. It was covered when not in use to preserve it for the next year. An open fire was built in the pit and permitted to burn slowly to cook the pig thoroughly. Oak poles were extended over the pit. Then the pig was placed on a wire screen, seasoned with vinegar, salt, and hot red peppers, and cooked slowly until done. At certain intervals the pig was turned over to eliminate too much browning on one side.

The pig tail was the first part of the pig to get done. Daddy would break the tail off and give me a piece of it. Pig tails tasted good — just like fresh barbecue. The pig cooked most of the day perfuming the air with a sweet barbecue aroma. When completely cooked, the barbecued pig was placed in a wooden tub and secured on the back porch or in the pantry, if one was available. As barbecue was needed, it would be sliced, chopped, and warmed in a black iron frying pan.

Meats for holiday dinners included baked hens, barbecue, beef stew, fried chicken, fried ham, fried fish, and steak. Breakfast meats were fried ham and side meats, homemade sausage, fried bologna, and fried steak with gravy. Eggs, fried sweet and white potatoes, grits, and corn fritters were regular breakfast foods. Usually, corn bread and biscuits were served with each meal. Egg bread, which tastes like plain cake, was a specialty for dinner. It was made with eggs, meal, self-rising flour, sugar, shortening, milk or water, and baked in a large baking pan. Rice and gravy were eaten with many meals.

Ma and Daddy permitted me to eat as much as I liked during the holidays, a rare treat reserved for Christmas time. During this time snowbirds got a rest from my trapping them and the fireplace received a little rest from baking on hot ashes and coals.

It was amazing how Santa always left tracks of himself, his sleigh, and his reindeer in the snow on the housetop. I tried to visualize how he and his eight reindeer landed so quietly I could not hear them. I could hardly sleep wondering just what Santa was going to leave me. Most of the time I was amazed at how very quietly Santa worked. But a few times I recall hearing apples and oranges fall on the floor while Santa was filling Christmas orders. Then I would close my eyes and try to fall asleep. I did not want Santa to know that I was awake!

Shoe boxes played a big role in our Christmas celebrations. Ma and Daddy bought us new shoes a few days before school opening in the Fall. The good shoe boxes were saved to set out for Santa Claus to fill. We were given special instructions to go to bed early on Christmas Eve. This was necessary to allow the fire in the bedroom to have enough time to burn out so that Santa was not burned coming down the chimney. This was one occasion when I willingly obeyed. Shoe boxes were arranged in a line on the floor of Ma and Daddy's room and had a note to Santa stuffed inside. Santa could identify each box by reading the hand written notes. I made sure I wrote down everything I wanted and explained how good I had been.

Long stockings were hung on the backs of chairs. I could hardly wait to get up, go in Ma and Daddy's room to find out just what Santa had left. I told Daddy and Ma over and over just what I wanted Santa to bring. I hoped they had not forgotten any of the things I mentioned to them. Fortunately, Santa always left enough of the things I requested to make me happy.

When I woke up on Christmas mornings I found apples, oranges, bananas and tangerines in the stockings. The shoe boxes were filled with candy canes, mixed candies, fresh grapes, dried seeded raisins attached to stems, animal crackers, nuts, and small toys such as harps and horns. Games such as checkers, Chinese checkers, and dominoes were left across the top of the boxes. Gloves, scarves, stockings, coats, and sweaters were also left next to each box.

I remember getting a small set of the characters in the book, *The Wolf and Three Pigs*. I thought that they were candy. When I ate a candy animal, I would take small bites to make the candy last longer. Surprisingly, when I bit the nose of the wolf it was hard and remained attached to the head. I made a terrible face, but learned an important lesson: "Examine what you have before biting it."

I sampled as much of the edibles as my stomach could possibly hold while waiting for Christmas breakfast, which would be served later than usual. This traditional breakfast was always oyster stew and crackers.

My parents enjoyed Christmas time, too! Daddy bought a Santa Claus suit with a long beard attached which he always wore when he told folktales on Christmas mornings. And Ma enjoyed cooking Christmas goodies.

By the end of the holiday season, Ma and Daddy were worn out! Since we spent most of the time in the house due to extremely cold weather, Ma and Daddy had more work to do—cooking and disciplining.

After two weeks of Christmas vacation, I was ready to return to school. I longed to work towards their dream of making a teacher out of me.

With my hands on my hip, I posed with the Brick Tri-County High
School Newspaper Staff in 1940, where I served as the Editor-in-Chief.
(Left to right): Mildred Wiggins, Joseph Stovall, me,
Andrew Howington, Willie Mae Cofield, Jesse Bolling,
Mary Lou Stovall, and Mrs. Carraway, the advisor.
Photo from the author's collection

•

chapter seven

School Days

During my childhood, my family moved frequently— a tiring task. We packed our belongings on a wagon with extended high sides. Mules and horses pulled the wagon down the long country dirt roads, as we sought out another farm and house. It was a welcome relief when we found a new farm to work. Unloading our wagon we moved into another worn down, unpainted house.

The farms we worked on were near the towns of Tarboro, Leggett, and Whitakers. Leggett was a small town with about four country stores and a garage. Whitaker was a little larger than Legett. There were more stores, a post office, cafeterias, and more people. Tarboro was the largest town. It had a hospital, post office, police station, stores, and all the conveniences of a large town.

Due to our constant moving I attended three different elementary schools: they were Leggett Colored School, Logsboro School, and Enfield Graded School. When I began elementary school in 1930, all the schools were segregated. It would be another 26 years before the Supreme Court ruled that segregation of public schools was unconstitutional (Brown vs. The Topeka Board of Education, 1954). For now, Jim Crow laws kept blacks and whites separate and unequal.

I remember walking to school, while the white children were

carried in bright yellow school buses. As the school bus drove by us, some of the children threw paper at me from the bus windows and called me names. I was taught to never retaliate. The Bible scripture, which states "Do not return evil for evil (Romans 12:17)," was ingrained in my mind.

Although I was often told I was a bright child and I had a great desire for reading, I experienced discipline problems at Logsboro School. My third grade teacher whipped me three times. However, I could not figure out why.

One day while playing during recess period, a boy threw a can of water on my starched dress. I cried because I knew my dress had to be worn more than one day and I could not wear it wrinkled. As soon as my teacher discovered why I was crying, she broke a branch from a nearby tree and pulled off the leaves to make a switch. Then she ordered the boy and me into the coat closet and whipped us with the switch.

On another occasion while I was sitting with a fellow student to help him with an assignment, he pushed me on the floor. Embarrassed and hurt I cried again. Ignoring the fact that she gave me permission to assist him, the teacher escorted us into the coat closet where she whipped us again with a switch.

On the third occasion, I was late for school because Ma overslept. When Ma arose, she insisted on making breakfast and lunch. Since there were no school lunch programs in the 1930s, we could not walk the long distance to school without eating breakfast. As soon as I walked into the classroom late, the teacher grabbed a yardstick and paddled me.

Logsboro School was funded by a wealthy Jewish man named Mr. Rosenwald, whom I think funded the school because he wanted all children to have nice schools to attend. Each morning we sang a song expressing our gratitude to Mr. Rosenwald. I was proud of the school's attractive appearance. All Rosenwald supported schools were built from the same architectural design and were painted white.

During the beginning of the fourth grade we moved again and I transferred to Leggett Colored School, a school whose structure was made of weather boards painted a dark reddish color. Upon entering the building, there was a long hallway leading to two classrooms in the back of the building. A classroom and a kitchen for teachers to prepare meals were on the left side of the hallway. To the right was a classroom and a large coat closet. The classrooms in the back had a stage in the front and were separated by a moveable partition. They were used for special programs or parent-teacher meetings. All the rooms were heated with wood and coal heaters. The boys took turns filling the heaters with wood and coal, and mopping the soot from the floors.

Mrs. Olive Eason became my fourth grade teacher, teaching me in grades fifth, sixth, and part of seventh. I admired Mrs. Eason. She was so pretty and her pleasant personality was a perfect match. She stressed good study habits such as: listening, following directions, completing homework assignments, using time wisely, and looking words up in a dictionary. I made straight A's in her classes!

Not only did Mrs. Eason challenge me academically, she gave me the first opportunity to fulfill my parents' "hands of a teacher" prophecy. In the Edgecomb County schools I attended, substitute teachers were not called when a teacher was absent. So whenever a teacher who taught a lower grade was absent, Mrs. Eason sent me to the classroom to serve as the "substitute teacher" for the day. I never received any pay for substituting for the teachers. But standing in front of the classroom looking in the innocent faces of the children as I taught them, inspired me. It was the beginning of "making a teacher out of me."

When I returned to my classes, sometimes the children would not play with me or Buddy. Buddy was called the teacher's "pet dog," and I was called the teacher's "pet cat." The children were probably envious of the extra attention we received from our teacher. Buddy was given the responsibility of starting the fire in the classroom heaters, and I was repeatedly called on to help students with their lessons. Although my classmates' name calling and refusal to play with us hurt my feelings, I was content playing with children from other classes during recess time.

I was not always kind to the other children. I remember stepping on a boy's bare feet because I thought he was cheating Buddy while playing marbles. The boy returned to class crying. Between his sobs and gulps, he explained what happened to the teacher. When he finished, Mrs. Eason looked at me and said, "Alfreda, I want you to stay after school."

While waiting for the school day to end, I wondered what Mrs. Eason was going to do. I hoped she would not send a bad note home to Ma and Daddy. If she did, Ma would get a switch and hit me on my legs. In those days whenever a child was punished at school, another punishment was usually given at home. Misbehaving was simply not tolerated!

When the last school bell rang I started screaming, fearing the worst. When I calmed down, I found out she only wanted to talk to me. "It's not nice to step on someone's bare feet with your shoes on," she said. Then she let me leave. Thank goodness. She did not write a note!

Elementary schools throughout the county held competitions in the areas of math, reading, and physical fitness. The academic competitions included solving math problems and reading from flash cards, and were held in different schools. The physical competitions included games like sack races, jumping rope, tug of war, and carrying peanuts in a spoon races. The games were held at the fairground in Tarboro. I participated in these competitions from second to seventh grades. I would get so excited anticipating the competitions, I often lost my voice.

It was during these times I grew to hate the color red. It started when my aunt gave me a red dress. Ma insisted that I wear this dress to the academic competition. However, I didn't like the dress because it clung to my thin body and made me look even skinnier.

To make matters worse, I wore plain white tennis shoes with laces that the kids jokingly referred to as "butter cookies."

While working math problems at the chalkboard, people yelled, "Look at the girl in the red dress!" Although I was successful and won many math and reading competitions, I was so embarrassed by the comments about my red dress that I never wore red again until twenty years later! As for the sack races or picking up peanuts with a spoon, I didn't have much success. But the fun I had competing made up for my losses.

In 1937 we moved to Enfield, where I attended seventh grade at Enfield Graded School for three months. There are two things that I remember about the school. First, it was a very large one story building. Secondly, it was the school I was attending when Ma died.

One cold winter day while Ma was outside cooking lard over an open fire, she became ill. After two weeks of battling pneumonia, a lung virus, she died peacefully at our home. Daddy was also suffering with pneumonia at the same time Ma was sick. Thank God he recovered! But, when Ma died, Daddy was too ill to make any arrangements. So, our family and friends planned the funeral.

Ma's funeral was held at Bethlehem Baptist Church. Reverend Clark, the pastor, conducted the service. It was the first funeral I ever attended. Back then children were not allowed to attend funerals until they were twelve years old. Since I was thirteen, I could attend. I wore a long sleeve, print rayon dress, black low heel shoes, and black socks.

Throughout the service I cried, as I thought about how much I would miss Ma. My life would never be the same without Ma's hearty laugh and loving ways. Reverend Clark saw me crying and comforted me. "The Lord will love and care for you," he soothingly assured me.

Ma was laid to rest near the church in a cemetery called "Old Apple Orchard," When we returned home, Daddy, who had been too sick to attend the funeral, did not even realize that Ma had been buried! As he suffered from pneumonia, I became very worried. Pneumonia had just claimed Ma's life. I hoped I would not lose both of my parents. Thoughts of becoming an orphan lingered in my mind until Daddy recovered.

After Ma's death Daddy had to make big adjustments to manage the home and farm. We moved back to the Leggett Colored School district where I finished elementary school.

About a year later Daddy married a lady named Florence, who was about 40 years old and had never been married. I was surprised because Daddy had not known Florence long and she was nothing like Ma. Florence was much taller and bigger than Ma. She had brown skin, like Daddy's, and short, bushy hair.

I could not call Florence "Ma," so Daddy said I could call her Miss Florence. I tried to be friendly to Miss Florence, despite the fact that I was not happy. I missed Ma so much. I felt uncomfortable around Miss Florence. It was like having a stranger in the house. Miss Florence was often quiet, as she tried to adjust to the demands of managing a family of eight children. In the end, it proved to be too much for her. About a year after Daddy and Miss Florence were married, she packed her bags and moved back in with her family.

Around the same time Miss Florence left I was finishing elementary school. Daddy said that since I was so smart, I could stay out of high school for a year or two. I was so hurt. All of my girlfriends were going to high school. I could not bear the idea of them progressing ahead of me. But Daddy needed help harvesting crops and picking cotton.

Miraculously, my poor farming habits improved. Three weeks after school opened very little cotton was left for picking. Buddy and Hazel knew how badly I wanted to go to school, so they offered to pick my share of the remainder of the cotton.

During the fourth week of school, I got up early every morning and knocked on Daddy's door. "Daddy, may I go to school today?" I asked. He did not reply because he had already told me

My certificate of promotion from elementary school to highschool, 1938. I had to beg Daddy to let me go to highschool during harvest season.

I could miss at least a year from school. Knowing that Daddy slept with a gun under his pillow to protect the household from convicts who frequently broke away from chain gangs made me a little nervous about knocking on his door. But I kept the words he and Ma said about "making a teacher out of me" in my heart, and I was determined to achieve my goal. If knocking on Daddy's door every morning could wear him down, I would do it.

After a week of knocking on Daddy's door, my "teacher looking hands" were feeling very sore. So I knocked lightly on the door the first Monday of the sixth week of school. To my surprise, Daddy's door flew open. Convinced that I would not cease knocking on his door, he yelled, "Get out of here and go to school before you lose your mind!" Excited, I quickly ate breakfast, dressed, and ran to the bus stop, which was about a mile from our house.

Six weeks into the school year I enrolled in Brick Tri-County High School, the same school Ma had attended. Since my sister Lillie was a junior, I had read her books. Sometimes Lillie was so tired from house and farm work that she was too tired to read in the evenings. So I read her books to her which made it easier for me to catch up. When I enrolled in school the books had not changed. At the end of my first three weeks of high school I made the honor roll. I remained on the honor roll every month for the remainder of my high school years.

One year the math teacher left school early and an English teacher was hired to fill her position until the end of the school year. Every day during my free period, the new math teacher asked me to go over the math lessons for the next day with her. Imagine that! I was teaching the math teacher how to do math. But I did whatever I had to do because I always remembered my parents' words "We're going to make a teacher out of you."

While a student at Brick Tri-County High School, I always took my assignments seriously, setting high standards for myself. Once in home economic class, I made a dress. Since I didn't have a pair of pinking shears, a special pair of scissors used for cutting and decorating seams, I pinked each seam with regular scissors. My teacher was so impressed with the seams, she displayed the dress on the wrong side for the other students to view. I refrained from boasting because Ma and Daddy often said, "When you do something well, it will be recognized by others."

They were right because my classmates noticed my achievements and often asked me for help. Many mornings as my school bus pulled up in front of the school, I would see them anxiously waiting for me to get off the school bus so I could help them with their homework assignments.

I was encouraged to be a well rounded student, so I participated in essay and history contests, basketball and school plays. During my senior year I had the lead role in the play, "Jane Eyre."

An award of merit from that National Youth Administration Program, May 14, 1941, seven months before the bombing of Pearl Harbor.

The final scene ended with a kiss between the leading male and female characters. When the leading male character told me he was really going to kiss me, I made sure I turned my head forcing him to kiss my hair. It was a hilarious ending!

I was not aggressive about dating in high school. Although I was friendly towards boys, a serious relationship never developed. Perhaps they stayed away after they saw the final scene in the "Jane Eyre" play.

With 29 students in my senior class, I graduated from Brick Tri-County High School in 1942. I was the class valedictorian. Soon after graduating I moved to Newport News, Virginia full of enthusiasm. I was awarded a full academic scholarship to Hampton Institute, a prominent college in Hampton, Virginia. I would be the first of my siblings to earn a college education.

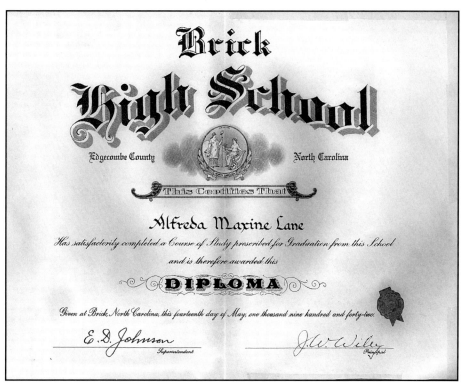

Brick
High School

Edgecombe County   North Carolina

This Certifies That

Alfreda Maxine Lane

Has satisfactorily completed a Course of Study prescribed for Graduation from this School
and is therefore awarded this

DIPLOMA

Given at Brick, North Carolina, this fourteenth day of May, one thousand nine hundred and forty-two.

E. D. Johnson
Superintendent

J. W. Wiley
Principal

My high school diploma, 1942. There were 29 students in my
graduating class. I was the valedictorian.

My childhood mentors were Ma and Daddy, who instilled a
dream and determination in me; and Mrs. Eason, my favorite elementary school teacher who stimulated me academically.

After spending seventeen years on the farm, I wondered what
it would be like living in the city. I was about to find out!

part two

The Dream Fulfilled

My "Lena Horne" pose. *Photo from the author's collection.*

•

chapter eight

The Early Days In Newport News, Virginia

I moved to Newport News, Virginia in 1942 soon after World War II was declared. Newport News, a small city in southeastern Virginia, had a thriving downtown district surrounded by rural areas. The city of Warwick, which merged with Newport News in 1956, was on the northern border. The city of Hampton, home of Hampton Institute, was on the southern border.

Whenever people left the south to come north, they usually lived with a relative until they found a job. I lived with my cousins. It was only going to be temporary until I enrolled at Hampton Institute in the Fall.

Lillie, my oldest sister, had already married and moved to Newport News. My youngest brother, Linwood, who was six, lived with her. Buddy was also living in Newport News and working at the Newport News Shipyard.

At first I wasn't fond of living in the city. Everything was different. I missed the familiar surroundings and faces in Leggett and Tarboro. But I learned to adjust to my new environment.

World War II was a few months old and many of the men around my age were drafted into the armed services. More job opportunities were open to women. It was not uncommon to see women driving cabs, painting houses, and working at gas stations and in the shipyard.

I looked forward to beginning my studies at Hampton Institute. My parents' dream of "making a teacher out of me" was so close. I could see myself standing in front of my class giving assignments, just as I had when a teacher was sick and Mrs. Eason sent me to the class to substitute. The weeks of knocking at Daddy's door begging him to let me go to school were going to pay off. I was about to begin studying for a degree in elementary education. And in four short years I would become a teacher!

During the summer of 1942, the unthinkable happened. Daddy, who had left the farm and come to Newport News to start a barber shop, became terribly ill with a virus. He would need financial help for awhile to make ends meet. So I decided to get a job to help out. After all, I could enroll in school next year. One year would not make too much of a difference, I reasoned as I began looking for a job.

I applied for a job as a clerk at a drugstore. Then one day I got a call from Nachman's Drug Store and I was offered the clerk job. After working for a few months I rented a room with a family in the Orcutt Homes section of Newport News.

Millions of young men were drafted in 1942. "Wait until the war is over and find a good service man!" was the mind set of many of my peers. Since I was not anxious to be in a relationship, I went along with them.

I kept putting off enrolling in college. There always seemed to be a good reason to wait another year. Pretty soon three years had passed and World War II was ending. I began to give more consideration to dating.

One Sunday while visiting Carver Memorial Presbyterian Church in Newport News, a girlfriend introduced me to a young man named Samuel Alexander. Everyone called him "Dickie." Very handsome with chocolate brown skin, he stood five feet, ten inches tall just like Daddy. My girlfriend said that Dickie graduated from Hampton Institute and was a World War II veteran. We exchanged hellos and went our separate ways. But for some reason, I could not forget him.

Samuel "Dick" Alexander, at 21.
Like Daddy, he was "tall, dark, and handsome."
Photo from the author's collection

There was a community center in the Newsome Park section of Newport News. On Saturday nights, chaperoned dances were held to provide entertainment for active and discharged service men. The community center had a large room that was reserved for dancing. The room was usually filled with cigarette smoke.

Smoking was popular, so electric fans were strategically placed throughout the recreation center to clear the air. A local band cranked out "One O'clock Jump," "Tuxedo Junction," "Take the 'A' Train," "Lets Go Do the Hop," "Autumn Leaves," and "I'll Be Seeing You," as young people did the hop, jitterbug, two step, waltz and slow drag up and down the dance floor.

One evening I joined my friends from the neighborhood who were going to the community center for an evening of dancing. When we arrived, I noticed Dickie standing by himself. I was happy to see him. He recognized me and walked over. We talked, then he asked me to dance. He was a good dancer, clowning around as we danced. "Since your name is Samuel, why are you called "Dickie?" I asked. "I had a cousin named Richard whom I resembled so much that my parents called me "Dickie," he replied quietly.

Although Dickie was charming, it was not love at first sight. We were both on the rebound. I was just looking for someone to "pal around with." And Dickie wasn't anxious to get in a serious relationship. We exchanged phone numbers and said good night.

After a few months, Dickie started calling me and we began dating occasionally. We went to movies, dances, parties, the beach, and to visit family and friends. I enjoyed dating Dickie, who had a good sense of humor.

The more we dated the more Dickie opened up to me. He shared that he had been a platoon sergeant in the army. While serving in Italy, he was hit by exploding shrapnel. He had completed an extensive recuperation period. As a result of his injuries he had a steel jaw, shoulder replacements, and shrapnel wounds on his arms and legs and an injured left eye. Plastic surgery had successfully concealed his facial wounds. But the wounds on his arms and legs, which looked like burn scars, were still apparent.

Dick in his army uniform in 1944, while serving as a
Platoon Sergeant in Italy during World War II.
Photo from the author's collection

Dick and me on a date in 1951. We only had eyes for one another.
Photo from the author's collection

Dickie was working as a delivery carrier for the <u>Journal and Guide</u> newspaper in Newport News. About a year later he accepted a job as a mail carrier with a Newport News branch of the United States Post Office.

One night after attending a movie, Dickie drove me home as usual. But when I reached for the door handle to get out of the car, he stopped me. He then announced, "It's time for us to get married!" We had been dating for a few years. He was thirty and I was twenty-six, so we were old enough, he reasoned. Although I was taken by surprise, I agreed. But there was one condition. "You have to ask my father for his permission," I said. I was sure Daddy would say, "Yes." After all, Dickie was a good catch; he had good character traits that would make him a good husband. Furthermore, he was from a good, stable family, and was college educated, and a World War II veteran.

Dickie felt nervous about asking my father's permission to marry me. He had another idea. He would buy the engagement ring and get the marriage license. Then we would go visit Daddy and let him know our intentions. Surely Daddy would say, "Yes." Around the end of March, 1951, Dickie slipped a diamond engagement ring on my wedding finger. It was a diamond solitaire that Dickie had allowed me to pick out. I was thrilled with the ring! As we drove over to Daddy's house, I kept looking down to admire the ring that adorned one of my "hands of a teacher."

When we arrived Daddy didn't notice the ring on my finger, so Dickie gave him the marriage license. Daddy looked over the marriage license, rolled it up and put it in his shirt pocket. Dickie and I were speechless. About five minutes later, Daddy removed the marriage license from his coat pocket, gave it to Dickie and said, "You have my blessings."

Daddy's only request was that we get married on a week day. He owned and operated a local barber shop and the weekends were his busiest days. "If you want me to give you away, you must get married on a weekday," he said. We decided to have a small, evening wedding on Wednesday, April 18, 1951.

As I prepared for my wedding day, I began to reflect on my life. I had been in Newport News for nine years, yet the "hands of a teacher" prophecy remained unfulfilled. I had nearly given up on my plans to enroll in college. Instead I was making $19.00 weekly as a checker at Modern Cleaners.

My only hope was that, perhaps, Dickie would agree to allow me to go to college. Education was important to his family. He and his brother and sister were college educated; therefore, I hoped he would approve. But I was uncertain. What if Dickie preferred a more traditional family life. I tossed these thoughts around in my mind as I prepared to become Mrs. Samuel Alexander.

91

Dick and me on our wedding day, April 18, 1951.
From the author's collection.

•

chapter nine

Married Life

Dickie and I decided to get married in Newport News at the home of his minister, Reverend J. Metz Rollins. The wedding was attended by my father, Arterway Lane; Dickie's parents, Mr. and Mrs. Roscoe Alexander; Dickie's sister, Mamie Lawton; and my oldest sister Lillie and her children; my youngest brother, Linwood; and Mrs. Rollins, the pastor's wife. My girlfriend, Odessa Johnson, was the bridesmaid and Mr. Alexander, Dickie's father, was the best man. Mrs. Alexander invited about a half dozen of her close friends.

It was a small, quiet wedding, exactly as I wanted. I never liked fanfare so Dickie complied with my wishes. We exchanged wedding vows on a beautiful spring night. I wore a beige suit and Dickie wore a navy blue suit.

We spent our wedding night at my sister, Lillie's house.We had planned to go to Chicago for our honeymoon, but postponed the trip until June. His brother, Alphonso, was graduating from McCormick Seminary in Chicago in June. We decided to make our trip to Chicago a celebration of our honeymoon and Alphonso's graduation.

After the wedding, Dickie shared more with me about his army career and childhood. While growing up his parents had wanted him to become a doctor.

Dick and me in Chicago during our honeymoon.
Photo from the author's collection.

He shared their dream and majored in math and chemistry in college. As fate would have it, he was drafted soon after graduating in 1942. After getting wounded, he decided against going to medical school, due to his war injuries. Fearing that he would be given an artificial eye, Dickie never told the military doctors that his left eye was badly damaged when they examined him. But I suspected that Dickie was nearly blind in his left eye. When we took trips out of town to visit friends and relatives, I noticed that Dickie closed his left eye while driving. When I asked if he were tired of driving, he always answered, "No."

During the first three years of our marriage, we lived in Dickie's parents' house, a large two-story structure located on

Marshall Avenue in Newport News. Back then Marshall Avenue was a very affluent neighborhood and I felt proud to live there with my new family. I immediately began calling my in-laws, "Daddy" and "Ma." Dickie's sister, Mamie, also lived in the house. Mamie was an elementary school teacher; her husband, Harold, taught tailoring at North Carolina A&T University in Greensboro, North Carolina.

Everyone got along well. My new "Ma" opened her kitchen to me so I could show of my cooking skills. I took pride in making recipes I learned on the farms in Edgecomb County. Dickie liked my cooking, but he refused to eat chitterlings!

Dickie continued working as a mail carrier, and I returned to my job at Modern Cleaners. Our first years of marriage were very happy.

About a year and half after our wedding, I discovered I was pregnant. Dickie always wanted one child— a son! On August 4, 1953 his wish came true. We had a beautiful baby boy whom we named Samuel Alexander, Jr. He had a head full of long, wavy, black hair, and looked like Dickie and me. The only noticeable difference was his fair complexion. Sometimes Dickie's friends would tease him about the baby's light complexion which bothered Dickie, but not me. I understood how genes work. My mother's father was white, and my mother had a light complexion. Hence, our son had inherited his grandmother's skin color.

For two months everyone referred to Samuel Jr. as "the baby." I did not think "the baby" was a good name. So Dickie and I decided to call our son, "Dickie," and I would call him "Dick." My in-laws never got used to this name change and still referred to my husband as "Dickie", and called my son "Little Dickie."

When I became a mother, Dick and I agreed that I should remain at home with Dickie to provide early childhood training. Again, my plans to earn a college degree were put on the back burner. Having been accustomed to working throughout the years, I began working at home. My mother-in-law noticed that many people were decorating with lace curtains, tablecloths, and slip-

The mother-to-be in 1953. Dick only wanted one child, a boy.
Photo from the author's collection.

Dick holding our new baby, Samuel Alexander Jr., in August, 1953.
Photo from the author's collection.

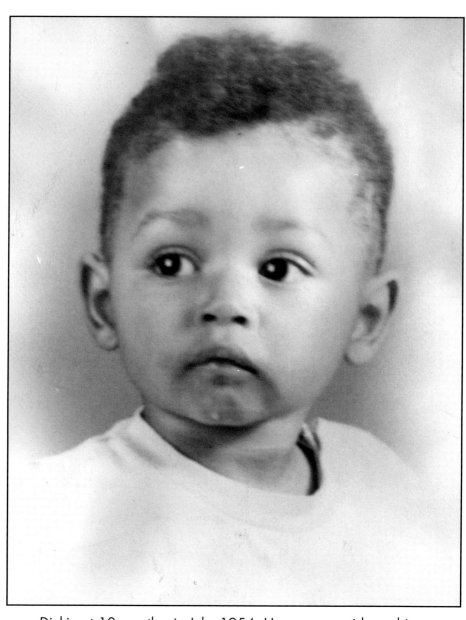

Dickie at 10 months, in July, 1954. He was my pride and joy.
Photo from the author's collection.

Dickie at two wearing his favorite straw hat, 1955.
Photo from the author's collection.

Dickie with Santa Claus, 1956.
Photo from the author's collection.

covers. She taught me how to iron and stretch these items. As a result I was earning a pretty good income and even saving some of the money.

In 1954, Dick and I moved into our first home, a white cottage style house with a white picket fence and a double garage. There were five rooms in the house and a big backyard for Dickie. It was located on 32nd Street in a quiet, well kept neighborhood on the east end of Newport News.

Daddy's third wife, Mattie Kearney,
Photo courtesy of Mattie Sutton

In 1956, Daddy remarried for the third time. His new wife was Mattie Kearney, a young woman about 30 years younger than he. Mattie was from Edgecomb County, too. I remembered her from elementary school, although I was a few years older than Mattie.

Mattie had grown up to be an attractive woman. She was about five feet, three inches tall, with brown skin, and short, black hair. Despite their age difference, she and Daddy got along very well. I was delighted to see Daddy so happy again, and I grew to love Mattie, too. Since she had grown up in Edgecomb County, we had a lot in common.

Dick was a great father. He loved Dickie and would take him to the park, beach, and to baseball games. This continued until Dickie was about five years old. When we went out as a family, we usually ate at the Cosmos Inn, a local restaurant and bar. There was a nice dining area in the front of the building and a bar near the back. The behavior on the premises was very acceptable and families with children often ate there.

As time passed I noticed that Dick did not always come directly home at the end of his work day. He would stop at the Cosmos Inn bar and remain there until it closed at 11:00 p.m.

I never worried about Dick going to bars. He had even taken me to them a few times. But I was worried that he was still in pain due to his war injuries. At work, Dick had been moved from his carrier position to a position which did not require lifting a heavy mailbag, due to his shoulder injuries. It hurt me to see Dick suffering. He was still a young man.

When Dickie was about six, I noticed Dick was drinking heavily. Unconsciously, he began to re-enact his army battles. He would often jump out of bed during the early morning hours and go through the motions of fighting on a battlefield. Then he'd fall back to sleep. Hours later when he awoke I'd mention it, but he could not remember his actions. His confusing behavior continued for about two years. I suffered in silence, afraid to tell anyone.

When Dickie started school, I decided to become the room mother for his first grade class. I visited the class regularly to assist the teacher, Miss Georgetta Manley, as needed. I also accompanied the class on field trips.

Miss Manley knew my in-laws and must have assumed I, too, was college educated. One day she asked me why I did not work as a substitute teacher. When I explained that I was not a college graduate, she informed me that I did not need a college degree to work as a substitute teacher. "It only requires college training," she said. She encouraged me to go to Hampton Institute and take a few courses. When I asked her to suggest a course, she recommended Methods which provides directions about how to teach.

I took her advice and decided I would take a few summer classes at Hampton Institute, so I could work as a substitute teacher. Dick and I had agreed that I stay home with Dickie during his formative years. Now that Dickie was in school, I hoped Dick would approve of me taking a few college courses and working occasionally as a substitute teacher.

The picture of me that Dick carried in his wallet.
Photo from the author's collection.

Me, as a college student in the early 1960s.
After 18 years of deferring my dream, I was about to fulfill
my parents' prophecy of "making a teacher out of me."
Photo from the author's collection.

●

chapter ten

College Days

Miss Manley's encouragement was just what I needed to rekindle my flame to become a teacher. In 1960, Dickie and I both enrolled in summer school. Dickie was six years old and was going to brush up on his math and reading skills. I was 36 and going to fulfill my parents' promise of "making a teacher out of me."

On registration day, quite a few teachers were changing their majors to Elementary Education because they were having difficulty finding jobs. I knew many of the teachers from church, social functions, and my neighborhood. I stood in line with them and turned in my registration slip just as they did, and like the others my registration was approved.

However, after two weeks of summer school, I was summoned to the office of Dr. Martha Dawson, head of the Elementary Education Department. I had no idea why she wanted to see me. When I arrived she informed me that she had discovered that I had no college credits. She quietly asked me, "Why are you taking Methods?" "My son's teacher suggested I take the course." I replied. "But there are many prerequisite courses that you should have taken before enrolling in Methods," she explained. Not fully understanding what she was talking about, I could only think of the adage "ignorance is bliss" as I sat listening.

Unknown to Dr. Dawson and me, Mrs. Marion Vassar, one of

The entrance of Hampton Institute in the early 1960s.
Photo courtesy of Hampton University.

my teachers, overheard our conversation from her office. Mrs. Vassar, who is now Dr. Vassar, raised her window slightly and suggested that Dr. Dawson give me a chance. "She's doing as well as the teachers who are changing their majors to elementary education," she said. Dr. Dawson gave in and allowed me to continue taking the Methods course. However, a week before summer school ended, I was summoned to her office again. I began to imagine what she would say. I feared she would say that I would not receive credit for the course because I had taken it out of sequence.

To my surprise, Dr. Dawson informed me that Mrs. Vassar and Mrs. Emma Bright, my other teacher, told her that I performed exceptionally well in their classes. "I plan to recommend you for a grant-in-aid," she began. "This will allow you to enroll as a full-time student. If you enroll, you must take courses in sequential order," she added.

Phenix Hall was the Education Building in the early 1960s.
Photo courtesy of Hampton University.

I left Dr. Dawson's office relieved and overjoyed. I would receive financial aid to continue college. Furthermore, I made A's in part one and part two of my Methods course. Finally things were looking up for me making me feel like I had moved further up this mountain called "teacher education."

Later, when I went to the registrar's office to register for the Fall semester, I spoke with Mr. Collis Davis, the registrar. He informed me that the school would grant me $900 for one year. I would be responsible for paying the other nine hundred dollars. I would also be expected to maintain at least a C+ average, preferably a B average.

I started thinking very seriously about college and Mr. Davis' comments. There were only 29 students in my high school graduating class. There would be over two hundred students in the Freshman class— students from all over the world. Dick's income was not enough to cover the mortgage and my tuition. But I had

$450.00 to pay for the first semester, so I took a chance and enrolled.

At the end of the first semester I made the dean's list. When Dr. Dawson found out she suggested that I go to the registrar's office to apply for scholarship aid based on my grade point average. I did and received enough aid to pay the entire tuition for the second semester.

After 18 years of deferring my dream of becoming a teacher, I was now on my way to fulfilling it. However, Dick was not happy about my good fortune. Although he did not forbid me to take the classes, he would often tell me I did not need to go to school. "Just stay home with Dickie," he said.

I was determined to finish college. I realized that Dick was probably drinking heavily to conceal the pain of his war injuries. Deep down I believed that one day Dick would be unable to work due to his injuries. I knew I had to be in a position to support our family financially, so I pursued my degree.

At the end of my first year of college, I noticed that Dick's behavior was growing worst. I decided I had concealed his behavior long enough. Although I was a bit frightened, I finally shared what was happening with my in-laws. Dick's parents discussed his behavior with him, but I did not notice any positive changes. Dick's parents probably understood him better than I. They had been with him during his recuperation period and observed the same unusual behavior. Fearing that Dick's recurring memories of his army battles might cause him to harm Dickie and me, his parents insisted that I leave Dick.

I prayed, hoping I would find the courage to leave Dick. It was a hard decision. I loved Dick. Where would I go? How would I explain things to Dickie? How would I finish college? I wrestled with these thoughts for four months. My in-laws kept encouraging me to leave Dick. Since I was already enrolled in college, they suggested that I finish college. They promised to take care of little Dickie. Although it meant breaking up my family, I decided to take their advice.

Harold and Mamie Lawton, my brother-in-law and sister-in-law, offered to keep Dickie until I graduated from college. They had just built a new three bedroom, ranch style home in Hampton. Mamie was teaching fifth grade and Harold was working at the post office in Newport News. They did not have children, and Dickie was so used to spending time with them. I was confident that they would provide a good home for Dickie and make excellent substitute parents. So I took them up on their offer.

One evening I called Mamie. She came over and picked up Dickie, and a suitcase of his clothes and toys. I moved to Hampton, where I lived with the Daughtry family. Etta Daughtry was one of my classmates. We spent a lot of time studying together and eating lunch at the campus grill. She was much younger than me, but when I confided in her she was very sympathetic. She explained my circumstances to her parents and they offered me free room and board until I finished college. Etta even sent her father to my house to help me move. I never said anything to Dick. His parents

My brother-in-law and sister-in-law, Harold and Mamie Lawton. They cared for Dickie for 3 1/2 years, while I attended Hampton Institute. *Photo courtesy of Harold and Mamie Lawton.*

My classmate, Etta Daughtry, and me. When I explained
my circumstances to Etta, she told her parents and they agreed to
let me live with them. *Photo courtesy of Mrs. Dorothy Daughtry.*

explained to him why I had left. Uncomfortable with living alone, Dick moved back to his parents' home.

As I expected, Dickie adjusted to living with his Aunt Mamie and Uncle Harold very well. He felt at home with them immediately. They often took him to visit me, his grandparents, and his daddy. Shortly after Dickie moved in with Mamie and Harold, Mamie took him on his first airplane flight. They went to Nashville, Tennessee, where Dickie visited his uncle and aunt, Reverend and Mrs. William Alexander, and his cousins. I had never flown on an airplane. As a result, Dickie was thrilled to know that he had experienced something that I had not.

Relieved that my son was happy and well cared for, I started adjusting to living with Mr. and Mrs. Henry Daughtry and their three children, Etta, Theresa, and Benjamin who was called "June". They accepted me graciously, and I began to feel like part of the family. I even referred to Mr. and Mrs. Daughtry as "Mama" and "Papa" Daughtry.

Mama Daughtry was an attractive, middle aged woman, with gray and black hair. She worked as an elementary school teacher in the Newport News Public School System. Papa Daughtry was tall and thin, and worked for an automobile wrecking company in Hampton. They always encouraged me to perform well in school.

Their daughters, Etta and Theresa, were also attending Hampton Institute. Every Monday morning Mama Daughtry placed money for bus fares and lunch on our bedroom dresser. She always left money for Etta, Theresa, and me. She and Papa Daughtry treated me with the same love and respect they gave their children.

I was amazed at how well the Daughtry children related to me. Although I had a good sense of humor, I was 18 - 21 years older. The years I spent with the Daughtry family were some of the happiest days of my life. The tight living arrangement never bothered me. I was so grateful! I knew I had to "crawl before walking," and I felt happy to be working toward my college degree. The child-

Mama Daughtry opened her home to me, and allowed me to live there rent free, while I attended college. Each week she placed lunch money and bus fares on the dresser for her two daughers and me. *Photo courtesy of Mrs. Dorothy Daughtry.*

hood dream of becoming a teacher was closer to being realized.

I remained on the dean's list the remaining three years at Hampton Institute, receiving financial aid to cover my full tuition until I graduated. I elected to attend summer school two summers, paying my own tuition.

Remaining on the dean's list, I was permitted to take extra courses. I graduated in January, 1964 summa cum laude earning a Bachelor of Science degree in Elementary Education. Although I made good grades, it required lots of dedication and constant studying. I did not have enough money to finance my college education. So I studied hard to keep my scholarship aid in tact.

While attending Hampton Institute I had three supervisors. Dr. Martha Dawson, Dr. Mary Christian, and Mrs. Marion Vassar, now Dr. Vassar. All of them encouraged me tremendously. Before graduating I wrote a poem titled, "A Tribute to My Supervisors" to recognize them and to summarize my goal of making a positive contribution to humanity. It reads:

A Tribute to My Supervisors

Gratitude

I want to thank the three of you
for being so gracious to me.
Your constant guidance and interest
have inspired me immensely.
I can't compose like Keats or Bryant,
Johnson, Shakespeare, Marlowe, or Poe
I'll resort to scanty expressions
to convey what I'd like you to know
I now feel as a minute branch
on the enormous "Education Tree,"
Whose roots have indulged deeply
to help others paddle the education sea.

Ogden Hall on the campus of Hampton Institute.
This is the building where graduation exercises were held.
Photo courtesy of Hampton University.

I do not wish my tiny branch
to cease when the most alert grow.
But stretch upward and outward
until the struggles begin to spark aglow.
I want to make a contribution
to humanity, as you see.
A long dream seems in the making,
Largely because of just you three!

On June 1, 1964 at 9:30 a.m., my graduating class formed a line outside of Ogden Hall on the campus of Hampton Institute to prepare for the commencement exercises. I was so excited, while standing in line! It had been more than thirty years since my parents had pulled me aside and compared my hands to those of a teacher. Their words "We are going to make a teacher out of you,"

Accepting my Elementary Education Degree on Graduation Day,
June 1, 1964. (Clockwise): Dr. Hugh Gloster, Dean of Faculty;
me, and Dr. Jerome Holland, President of Hampton Institute.
Photo from the author's collection

At last, my teaching degree!

flooded my mind. In a few moments I would be receiving a teaching degree.

Daddy and Dickie were waiting in Ogden Hall. They were anticipating seeing me march in adorned in my black cap and gown. When my name was called and I walked across the stage to accept my degree, they cheered me on. As I marched down the aisle to return to my seat, Dr. Beyma, my freshman math teacher, stood up and shook my hand. I smiled and thanked him. When I returned to my seat, I wondered why he had remembered me. It had been nearly four years since I took his class. When I opened the commencement program, I discovered I was one of the five students who graduated summa cum laude. I also received Departmental honors from the Elementary Education Department. An overwhelming joy bubbled up inside of me, as tears began to flow down my cheeks.

When the ceremony was over, the other graduates and I marched outside of Ogden Hall. Daddy, and Dickie were anxiously waiting for me. We stood there, kissing, hugging, and crying. I was so happy, I even kissed my diploma. Daddy hugged me and exclaimed, "I'm glad that you finished college!" Both of us laughed when I reminded him about the times I knocked on his door asking if I could go to high school.

Daddy died of heart failure in February, 1972. He was very pleased that I had fulfilled the dream of becoming a teacher. Thinking back, when I started teaching, I would stop by his barber shop almost every Friday to talk with him as he cut hair. He proudly told his customers, "That's my daughter, Freda. She's a teacher."

My first class at Thomas Jefferson Elementary School
in Newport News, Virginia, 1964-1965.
They were getting ready to square dance!
Photo from the author's collection

•

chapter eleven

Realized Goal

The goal of becoming a teacher materialized in January, 1964, the same month I completed the requirements for a Bachelor of Science degree in Elementary Education from Hampton Institute. I was hired to teach at Thomas Jefferson Elementary School in Newport News. Having been issued a temporary diploma, I kissed it leaving a large lipstick print on it and thanked God. My regular visits to the bathroom, where I would kneel by the dirty clothes hamper to pray for assistance with my studies, would be relaxed for awhile.

I knew the children in the first class I was assigned to very well. It was the same class that I taught while completing my student teaching requirements. Mrs. Naomi Grannum, Principal of Thomas Jefferson Elementary, was my supervisor during student teaching. She came to the classroom infrequently, leaving me alone in the classroom with the children most of the time.

Occasionally, she had conferences with me offering all the moral support I needed. The pupils were not told that I was student teaching. With maturity and having completed the first half of my student teaching at the Hampton Institute Non-graded Laboratory School, Mrs. Grannum allowed me to teach in the classroom with little supervision. Rather than sitting in on my

Hands of a teacher at work teaching arts and crafts
at the Jewish Community Center, 1965. *Photo courtesy of the
Jewish Community Center, Newport News, Virginia.*

class, Mrs. Grannum and I agreed that she would turn the listening device on in her office and listen throughout the day, whenever she felt it was necessary.

Many of the children were repeating grades and there were quite a few discipline problems. The teacher they had started out the year with had resigned after suffering an illness. Consequently, there had been many substitute teachers.

On my very first day I candidly announced to the students, "I am not a substitute teacher. I expect us to get along well." Knowing this would be my class for the remainder of the year, after completing student teaching, I decided to use every positive procedure to earn the students' respect and confidence.

Very little teaching was accomplished the first few days. I talked with the students to find out what they expected of me. I also told them what I expected from them. Although I did not agree with everything they expected, I encouraged them to take this opportunity to express themselves. We decided that we needed some acceptable classroom rules.

They helped make the rules, which I wrote on the chalk board. I was cautious to use positive terms, omitting the word "don't". The next day the rules were written on a very attractive chart which was placed on the classroom wall. Having been involved in making the class rules the children were motivated to follow them. I suggested that the rules be displayed for two weeks and then taken down. The class happily agreed.

We soon established a friendly, compassionate bond. I ate lunch with my class everyday, although there was a lunch table reserved for teachers. I made sure I gave them as much positive feedback as possible, telling them how pleased I was with their good behavior and to try harder when they behaved poorly.

At the end of the second week, there was a visible difference in the children's behavior and several people took notice. Mrs. Grannum, the principal, confessed that I had achieved what she thought was impossible to achieve throughout the remainder of the school year. Even a custodian asked me "What did you do with those children?" "I allowed them to become participants in establishing an acceptable order of behavior," I answered. I felt humble because it was the students who had established the rules of acceptable behavior and had adjusted their behavior accordingly. Once their behavior improved, we got to the tasks of studying and improving academically.

I learned many valuable lessons during my first year of teaching. The most important one was the value of building self-esteem. When you build self-esteem you help people feel good about themselves. When people feel good about themselves, you can expect better work habits. Everybody wants to be accept-

Me posing with students at the Hampton Institute Non-graded Laboratory School in 1965. *Photo from the author's collection.*

ed. Regardless of how limited a person may appear, I learned to always be kind to them. Most of them returned my kindness. I also learned to model self-control. Unknowingly, I became a mentor to several children. When the school year ended I resolved to transfer the lessons I learned to other classrooms and my dealings with people in general.

I had some great advantages over most recent college graduates. I tried to take advantage of my past experiences. I was mature, 18 years older than most graduates. I grew up in a large family, where I learned to share. I had a ten-year-old son, which gave me the opportunity to observe and learn firsthand about childhood behavior. Working quite a few jobs had taught me how to get along with people from many facets of life. I had also worked and taken care of myself for nine years before getting married.

In April, 1965 Dr. Jerome Holland, President of Hampton Institute, invited me to join the faculty as a teacher at Hampton Institute's Non-graded Laboratory School, where the emphasis was placed on skill development rather than grade level. He was impressed with the assignments I gave his daughter, Lucy, during my student teaching assignment at the Laboratory School. He assured me that I would receive money from Hampton Institute to continue graduate studies, as long as I returned to teach one year after attending graduate school.

I decided to continue my education at Indiana University. I went during the summers, driving alone to the campus located in Bloomington, Indiana which was more than 1,000 miles from my home in Hampton. Daddy remarked that it took a lot of nerves to drive that long distance and that he would not have done that as a young man. "You would have had a hard time driving a Model T Ford with a speed limit of 25 miles per hour to Indiana," I joked. We both laughed, feeling overjoyed that I had completed my undergraduate degree and was furthering my education.

Indiana University

School of Education

To all who may read these letters, Greeting:

hereby it is certified that upon the recommendation of the Faculty, the Trustees of Indiana University have conferred upon

Alfreda Lane Alexander

the degree of

Master of Science in Education

in recognition of the fulfillment of the requirements for this degree. In Witness Whereof, this diploma is given at Bloomington, Indiana. Dated August 31, 1968.

Attest: *Charles E. Harrell*
Secretary of The Trustees

President

David L. Clark
Dean

My Master's Degree from Indiana University.

Mrs. Naomi Grannum, the principal at Thomas Jefferson Elementary School, recommended me for a principalship at the end of my first year of teaching. However, I had to leave the Newport News Public School System in 1965 to fulfill my obligation to teach at the Hampton Institute Non-Graded Laboratory School.

My first year of putting my "hands of a teacher" to the test was a moving experience. I learned a lot from my first class. These lessons helped me with raising my own son.

Dickie and me in 1963, the same year President John F. Kennedy
was assassinated. *Photo from the author's collection.*

●

chapter twelve

A Single Parent in the 1960's

After I graduated from Hampton Institute, I bought a one story, brick house near the Aberdeen area of Hampton. Dickie, who was now eleven-years-old, came to live with me. Dickie had developed new interests. He enjoyed listening to the "Motown" music of the sixties, and played Little League baseball. Overall, he was the same obedient child.

In 1963 I filed for divorce from Dick. At first he resisted the divorce arguing that I would always be his wife. But, we decided to remain good friends and to work together to raise Dickie. Eventually, Dick accepted my decision and the divorce was finalized in 1964.

After living apart from Dickie I had to get use to having him around. One day Dickie and I went shopping on Washington Avenue in Newport News. While in Leggetts Department Store, Dickie left my side to look around in another area.

Forgetting that he was with me, I left and walked over to Broadways, a store three doors down the street. A few minutes later I felt a hand hitting me on my back. Astonished, I turned around. Dickie stood behind me crying, "Why did you leave me?" he sobbed, "I was going to the police station down the street to tell them that you went home and left me." I apologized and explained what had happened. Dickie said he understood. And I never forgot him again!

The 1960s and early 70s were turbulent times in American history. Dickie was growing up amidst the assassinations of President John F. Kennedy, Civil Rights leaders, Malcolm X and Dr. Martin Luther King, and presidential candidate, Bobby Kennedy. The Civil Rights movement was in full force. The drug laden, hippie movement was captivating millions of teenagers, and the Vietnam war was being fought.

In view of the fact I was a single parent, I enrolled Dickie in Boy Scouts and Sunday School to give him a moral and spiritual foundation. He sang in the church youth choir and was active in church sponsored programs. It worked! I never experienced any serious discipline or behavior problems. Dickie was responsible and independent. He studied on his own, got up on time to go to school, and went to school regularly. Whenever he had a problem, we talked about it and reached an agreement without arguing. I only remember whipping Dickie once—when he was four years old.

He was playing with a group of children near our home. I poked my head out the door and yelled for him to come home, but he did not respond. Upset that he had not obeyed me I came outside. And just as Ma used to do when I was a girl, I broke a small branch from a tree and walked down the street to where he was playing. When I reached him, I hit his legs a few times, and said, "When I call you, I expect you to come!" Dickie cried, claiming he did not hear me.

About two months later while cleaning his ear with a cotton swab, a huge lump of wax was dislodged from one of his ears. I told him I did not understand how he could hear with that much wax in his ear. He instantly proclaimed, "I told you that I did not hear you when you came down the street and whipped my legs that day." I felt so sorry for whipping him that day. When Dickie was older I mentioned that whipping to him. Although I did not think he was old enough to remember, he did!

During Dickie's adolescent years, I noticed that he poked out his lips and puffed up his jaws whenever I was discussing some-

Dickie serving as a junior groomsman at one of my friend's wedding.
Photo from the author's collection

Dickie wearing a "bush" in 1975.
Photo from the author's collection

thing with him that he did not like. On one such occasion, I said "Dickie, I realize you will not always agree with my expectations, but rather than poking your lip out we should talk about it." Soon after we had this conversation, I called him to the dinner table to eat. He came to the table but before sitting down, he turned the radio to a station that was playing rock and roll and soul music.

"Why do you have to listen to that kind of music?" I asked him. "Mother," he calmly replied, "you told me whenever I disagree with you we should talk. Every morning at breakfast time I listen to your music. I don't like it either, but I don't say anything. I am only going to be out here for thirty minutes. If I can listen to your music in the morning, I think it's fair for you to listen to music I like at dinnertime," he added. "You are absolutely correct," I replied, as the raspy voice of James Brown filled our home.

Besides music, other big issues during the 1960s and 70s were hairstyles, drugs, and flashy clothes. Long hair was "in." "All the kids are wearing their hair in an afro style. It's called the 'bush'," Dickie explained. He was upset because his grandmother and Aunt Mamie told him not to wear this new "bushy" hairstyle.

"Okay, you can let your hair grow long and style it in a 'bush' as long as you keep it clean and neatly shaped," I said.

We talked openly about widespread use of marijuana, LSD, and heroin. I explained the dangers of drug use to him. The danger of drugs was also being taught in Dickie's health classes at school, reinforcing my teachings.

One day Dickie came home from school and told me that his classmates had called him a "chicken," because he refused to smoke a funny looking cigarette that was being passed around. The other kids were taking a puff, but Dickie refused.

I was so proud of him! "People will criticize you and call you a chicken when you stand up for what is right," I explained. "As long as you're saying 'no' to something that you don't feel right about because it's not in agreement with your thinking, don't worry about it." I added.

As for clothes, platform shoes, big collar, multi-colored shirts, and wide leg pants dominated the fashion scene. I kept reminding Dickie not to dress too extravagantly, especially when going to school. Overall, I think Dickie managed well during these trying times. He made wise decisions and used good common sense.

Dickie attended Thomas Eaton Junior High School and Bethel High School in Hampton. Both schools had been integrated, as a result of Supreme Court decision that ruled segregation of public schools was unconstitutional. Dickie played in the school band and also played basketball. Although he grew to be six feet, five inches tall, he was not willing to give up band to concentrate on high school basketball.

Academically, Dickie did well in junior high school and was inducted into the honor society. However, his first high school report card was atrocious. His grades ranged from A's to D's. "What kind of report card is this?" I asked. "Mother, I have just entered high school. I need a little time to adjust. I'll do better next time," he promised. He kept his promise.

I never discussed going to college with Dickie. Growing up, he knew it was expected of him. Seeing me work hard to become a teacher had a positive impact on Dickie. However, he didn't want to attend Hampton Institute. Although Dickie was given the opportunity to apply to three colleges, he chose to apply to only one. His choice was Virginia State College, located in Petersburg, Virginia. When I asked why he only applied to one college, he said, "Sending three applications with fees seems like a waste of money." His logic proved correct because during the first semester of his senior year at Bethel High School, Dickie received notification of his admission to Virginia State College.

In June, 1971 Dickie graduated from high school. Dick and I were so pleased. Having remained close to Dickie over the years, Dick loved his son and wanted him to finish college and make a positive contribution to society.

During Christmas of 1972 while sitting at the kitchen table

Me, Dickie, and Aunt Mamie Lawton at Dickie's college graduation,
one of the happiest days of my life! Dickie graduated in 1975
from Virginia State College in Petersburg, Virginia.
Photo from the author's collection.

with me, Dickie proudly remarked, "Hey Mom, I've got something good going for me. You! There is nothing for me to do but be successful, when I see the achievements that you've made in such a short time. You set a good example for me."

Dickie performed well academically at Virginia State College, which made Dick and me very proud. We looked forward to his graduation in 1975. However, during Dickie's junior year of college, Dick died of kidney failure. He had taken an early retirement from the Post Office due to his illness. Dickie had been coming home on weekends and in the summers to spend time with Dick. I visited Dick too, sometimes making dinner for him. Watching his father's health deteriorate was painful for Dickie. When Dick died on April 8, 1974, we painfully accepted it and resolved to move on with our lives.

Dickie graduated from Virginia State College in May, 1975 with a Bachelor of Science degree in Business Administration. Seeing my son earn his college degree was one of the happiest days of my life. After graduating, Dickie moved to Washington D.C. to work in the Financial Office at Howard University. In 1979, he earned a Masters Degree in Business Adminisration and was transferred to the Purchasing Department. In 1986, Dickie became a Certified Purchasing Manager (C.P.M.). He is employed at Howard University, where he serves as Assistant Director for Procurement Services.

I was happy that immediately after graduating from high school Dickie was able to go to college and begin his career. I returned to college 18 years after graduating from high school. Although I got off to a slow start, my career moved fast.

Me, as principal at South Morrison Elementary School, 1982.
Photo from the author's collection

•

chapter thirteen

Becoming A Principal

I worked at the Hampton Institute Non-Graded Laboratory School for three years before returning to the Newport News Public School System in 1968. It had been 14 years since the Supreme Court ruled against segregated public school systems (Brown vs. Topeka Board of Education). The ruling was slowly but surely being implemented in school systems throughout the country. Newport News public schools were in the early phases of integration when I returned.

I was assigned to teach fourth grade at Hilton Elementary School in the Hilton area of Newport News. Hilton was an affluent white neighborhood. The school was located along the James River. There was a river bank nearby and I could look out of my window and see ships under construction at the Newport News Shipyard.

I enjoyed teaching at Hilton Elementary. Although I was the only black full-time teacher on staff for three years, I did not feel isolated. I chose to focus on achieving my teaching goals rather than skin color. I also became active in the Newport News Teachers Association, where I served as an officer before becoming appointed to the Board of Directors.

One of the problems with integrating school systems was that children attended the schools closest to their neighborhoods.

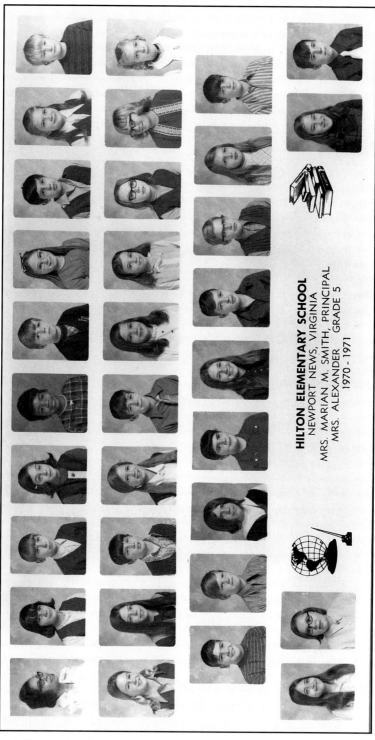

My fifth grade class at Hilton Elementary School in 1970-1971.
Photo from the author's collection

Since most neighborhoods were segregated, most schools were segregated. In 1971, busing was introduced to integrate public schools. Busing involved taking children out of their neighborhood schools and sending them to schools in different communities. Hence, white students were sent to schools in black neighborhoods, and black students were sent to schools in white neighborhoods. Busing bothered a lot of people. But I knew it was something that had to be done.

Teaching staffs were also integrated which was a hard transition for many teachers, who had grown accustomed to teaching segregated classes. Several of the teachers that I worked with approached me to ask me how I managed in an all white school. "I'm here to teach! I don't care what people think about me." I said. In the aftermath of the teacher integration I was moved to Denbigh Elementary School, which was in a middle class neighborhood surrounded by apartments and shopping centers.

At Denbigh Elementary School I became the Director of Patrols. Two students were selected from each class to serve as patrols. It was a real honor for a student to be selected for the patrol program! Patrols wore a silver badge on their shirt that looked like a police badge, and a sturdy white belt that hung over their shoulders and wrapped around their waists. They monitored the halls and bus areas before and after school to help maintain order. Whenever there was a behavior problem on the school buses, a patrol would bring the children to me to solve the problem before school opened.

Once a month I would meet with the student patrols to discuss the effectiveness of the patrol program. I asked them for suggestions on how to solve discipline problems. Although some of their suggestions were comical, most of them were practical. So I implemented them. The impact of their suggestions was evident to the principal and teachers. Very few students were sent to the principal's office.

In 1972 the Newport News School system decided to hire

assistant principals on the elementary level to assist with instruction and to help solve discipline problems.

Content with teaching, I was not interested in becoming an administrator. Therefore, I did not apply for an assistant principal position. However, the principal and several teachers noticed how well I got along with patrols and other students. One day I overheard some of my co-workers discussing their intentions to send my name to the personnel office for consideration for an assistant principal position. "No!" I pleaded. "I only want to teach."

When the school year ended I was asked to come back to the Central Administration Building, where I usually spent part of the summers evaluating books and other curriculum materials for the local board of education. But this year was different.

When I arrived I was invited into the office of George McIntosh, the Superintendent. Seated in the office were heads of departments and personnel members. After asking me to take a seat, the Superintendent said, " I heard that you do not want to leave the classroom." "Yes." I replied, still unsure why I had been invited to the meeting. "Well, the people in this office and I believe you would better serve the Newport News Public School system as an Assistant Principal," he announced.

I could not believe it! Looking down at my "hands of a teacher," I thought "I have only taught 5 1/2 years in Newport News." I had envisioned teaching for at least 25 years. How could my teaching career be coming to an end? I sat patiently at the table, still somewhat bewildered, as I carefully answered a round of questions about the problems an assistant principal may face. At the end of the conference, I was informed that my teaching days were over! In the Fall, I would become the Assistant Principal at South Morrison Elementary School. I did not know whether to laugh or cry. I knew I would have to accept the promotion. But when I went home I cried, because I hated to give up my children.

I reported to South Morrison Elementary School and, to my surprise, I felt right at home. Three of the teachers that I had worked

DENBIGH ELEMENTARY SCHOOL
Newport News, Virginia

1971-72

Mrs. Sarah B. Wright
Principal

Mrs. Alexander
Fifth Grade

My fifth grade class at Denbigh Elementary School, 1971 - 1972, where I worked as Director of Patrols. I was moved to Denbigh Elementary School as part of the teacher integration program. *Photo from the author's collection.*

with at Thomas Jefferson Elementary School were now working at South Morrison. It was so good to see familiar faces!

The principal, Tom Willis, was a few years my junior. He had light brown, curly hair and was tall, about six feet. Before becoming a principal he was a physical education teacher. Mr. Willis had great interpersonal skills and spent a lot of time listening to the teachers' concerns. We got along well.

As Assistant Principal, I assisted with supervising instruction to make sure that teachers' lesson plans were consistent with school learning objectives. I also supervised parent conferences and counseled children. When I had free time I helped with teaching, extending my "hands of a teacher" to several classrooms.

One of my fondest memories is of greeting students each morning as their buses arrived. I wanted to make sure the children were alert and ready to begin the school day. When I noticed that a child was cranky, I took him/her to my office to find out what was wrong. Most of the time it was because the student did not have breakfast. So I would take him/her to the cafeteria to eat before returning to class.

I worked full-time at South Morrison for two years. Then one day I was informed that I would be assigned to serve as Assistant Principal at another school, Sanford Elementary. I would alternate between the two schools. One week I worked two days at South Morrison and three days at Sanford Elementary. Then the next week I would work three days at Sanford Elementary and two days at South Morrison.

It was a big adjustment traveling back and forth between two schools. But I tried to make the most of it. Sanford Elementary School was in dire need of leadership. The assistant principal had been transferred to another school, and the principal had retired.

The new principal, Ken Bennett, and I started at Sanford around the same time. Mr. Bennett and I had met at the Newport News Principal Association meetings, so I felt comfortable around him from the very beginning. He was real tall, like a basketball player. He stood more than six feet tall, and had light brown hair.

Like Mr. Willis, he was a few years younger than me. However, his personality was different than Tom's. Ken Bennett was more reserved. But we got along well, too! I oversaw instructional programs and conferences with teachers, while he concentrated on maintaining the building's appearance and the overall operation of the school. He also assisted me with my responsibilities.

I continued alternating between both schools for three years, performing the same responsibilities at each school During this time, I would often think of Ma and Daddy's little verse:

All that you do,
Do it with your might.
Things done by halves
Are never done right.

Although, initially, I was not excited about becoming an assistant principal, I found the work rewarding. I still made time to teach. I was even assigned to assist the gifted classes at both schools. I also worked hard to maintain positive relationships with staff members, parents, and school support departments. Quite frequently I would hear the comment, "You should become a principal!"

A the end of the 1977 school year, I received a note from the new School Superintendent, Dr. Roberts, requesting a conference. I was not alarmed about the request because around the end of the year the Superintendent met with most administrators.

It had been a pretty ordinary day when I arrived for my meeting with Dr. Roberts. After giving me a warm greeting, Dr. Roberts informed me that he had just completed back to back conferences with both of my principals. "One left by the exit door and the other entered through the entrance door. They had no time to talk, yet they both said the same thing!" Dr. Roberts told me that Mr. Willis and Mr. Bennett both said that I had never brought any reports or

My staff during my first year as principal at South Morrison
Elementary School. I am seated in the first row on the left.
Photo from the author's collection

gossip about what was happening in the other school to their
respective school. "I think that is one of the nicest compliments that
could be offered a person." Dr. Roberts added. "They are two different people. I respected their individualities," I replied. Then
came the shock. "I have appointed you a principalship and I hope
you will accept it," he said.

My hands turned icy cold. My parents never discussed with me
just how far my "hands of a teacher" could go. I had only dreamed
of becoming a teacher. But I had come to understand that teaching
can reach beyond the classroom. Since so many people kept
telling me I had what it takes to be a principal, I decided I would
give it a try. "Yes. I accept." I happily answered. After assuring me
that I would do well, Dr. Roberts said I would be assigned to
Thomas Jefferson Elementary School, effective immediately!

I was overjoyed! Thomas Jefferson Elementary School was the

same school where I had embarked on my teaching career. Now thirteen years later, I would be returning to serve as the Principal. Since I had already planned a ten day vacation in Sacramento, California, Dr. Roberts agreed to let me take it. But first I had to report to Thomas Jefferson Elementary School and get settled in.

Memories of Mrs. Grannum and my first class flooded my mind, as I moved into my new office at Thomas Jefferson Elementary School. I had been a principal for three days when my vacation started.

While relaxing in sunny California I received a message to call Dr. Roberts, who had called my sister to find out how he could reach me. "What is it, Dr. Roberts?" I asked wondering what was so urgent that it could not wait until I returned.

Dr. Roberts informed me that Tom Willis was transferring to another school and some of the teachers at South Morrison had come to him requesting that I be assigned as the new principal. I was really surprised! "Would you have any problems assuming the role as principal at South Morrison?" Dr. Roberts asked.

"No" I said, still amazed by the teachers' reactions.

I returned from my vacation and in June, 1977 I became Principal of South Morrison Elementary School, after serving as the assistant principal for five years.

At the first staff meeting, I thanked the staff for the vote of confidence they had expressed when they went to Dr. Roberts on my behalf. I then held up one of Mr. Willis' shoes. "I may not be able to fill the shoes of Tom Willis. But I will do my best!" I exclaimed.

After becoming a principal, my job expectations varied. I continued to perform many of the same tasks I did as assistant principal. In the mornings I would stand by the bus area to greet the students. I still oversaw the teachers' lesson plans to make sure the learning objectives were being met. However, teaching the pupils was limited. As chief administrator of the building, I had new responsibilities such as evaluating staff performances, maintaining good public relations, and insuring that all policies regarding discipline techniques and parent/teacher relations were adhered to. I also planned fun activities for staff members, parents and students.

My students and staff called me Mrs. "A" which was short for Mrs. Alexander. There was generally a pleasant atmosphere at South Morrison Elementary. Although I was the principal, I always tried to remember to say "thank you." And like Ma and Daddy, I remembered to give praise whenever it was deserved.

After serving as a principal for six years, I decided to remarry in 1982. Little did I know a new husband would be the beginning of a whole new life.

Bill and me on our wedding day, December 12, 1982.
Photo from the author's collection

•

chapter fourteen

New Husband, New Life

My second husband, Willis R. Drummond, Sr., was called "Bill." He grew up in Pleasantville, New Jersey about six miles south of Atlantic City. Surprisingly, Bill's family moved to Newport News in 1942, the same year that I moved there. Bill's parents lived about a half of a block from Dick's parents. He graduated from Huntington High School in 1943, then joined the Navy to serve in World War II. After a three year stint in the Navy, Bill attended West Virginia State College where he majored in Mechanical Arts, which is now called Industrial Engineering.

Unable to land an engineering position locally, he held a civil service position as a mechanic at Fort Eustis Army Base in Newport News. However, he lost his job due to a reduction of civil service personnel. In 1953 he joined the Newport News Sergeant's Department, which became the Sheriffs Department in 1958 when Warwick County and Newport News merged becoming one city.

Bill spent the bulk of his career working in the Civil Office of the Sheriff's Department, where he served civil warrants and eviction notices. In 1970 he was promoted to Chief Deputy and his responsibilities shifted to personnel management.

It was the second marriage for both of us. Bill's first wife's name was Marilyn. They met in college and were married in

Bill Drummond Sr. in his Chief Deputy Sheriff's uniform in 1983. *Photo from the author's collection.*

1951, the same year Dick and I married. We were all members of the same church and we visited each other's home occasionally. Bill and Marilyn had their first child, Sheila, in 1953, the same year Dickie was born. Dickie and Sheila knew each other quite well, and often played together at church sponsored activities. When Sheila was six-years-old, Willis Drummond Jr. "Billy" was born.

In 1979, after 26 years of marriage, Marilyn died. Bill grieved for a year. Then, determined to go on with his life, he asked me out on a date. To our surprise, we realized we were fond of many of the same activities such as: watching television, going to movies, driving along scenic roads in the car, and visiting family and friends. We dated for about two years. On December 12, 1982 I became Mrs. Willis R. Drummond Sr. I was 58 years old and Bill was 57.

It snowed on our wedding day. We were married at Carver Memorial Presbyterian Church in Newport News. Our children and Bill's grandchildren attended the ceremony, along with a few of our close friends. Our children were happy about our marriage. Sheila served as my matron of honor, and Dickie was Bill's best man. Sheila and I wore pink dresses, and Bill and Dickie wore blue suits.

After the wedding ceremony, we drove to Afton Mountain, near Charlottesville, Virginia. It was still snowing when we pulled

Posing with my new family after exchanging wedding vows in 1982.
(left to right): Bruce, Sheila (holding Justin), Bill Jr., Freda
(standing behind Jae'Mie), Bill, and Dickie.
Photo from the author's collection

into the Holiday Inn. The employees of Holiday Inn sang wedding songs to us and ordered wine and cheese. During the entire weekend we were treated like royalty, receiving top notch service and free meals.

Due to the heavy snow, we stayed inside the hotel most of the weekend. Then we went to Charlottesville to do a little shopping and sightseeing. Later in the week we spent an exciting, enjoyable evening on the mountain top.

After a week long honeymoon, I moved into Bill's home in the Denbigh area of Newport News. It was a comfortable, six room, cottage style house, about eight miles from South Morrison Elementary School. Our only problem was combining two houses of furniture into one house. We ended up giving most of the unnecessary furniture to our children.

Bill and I shared household and yard responsibilities. I enjoyed cooking, while he took great pride in the lawn work. We both enjoyed music. Bill played the drums and saxophone. He had a variety of tapes and records by artist such as Miles Davis, Dinah Washington, John Coltrane, and Sonny Stith. Most of the time there was jazz music playing in our home.

By the time Bill and I married all of our children were grown and were college graduates. Sheila attended Lafayette College in Easton, Pennsylvania, where she majored in Psychology. She married a man she met at college named Bruce Hughes, who majored in history and economics and worked for the Equitable Life Insurance Company. Sheila went on to earn a Master's degree in Counseling Psychology from the University of Bridgeport in Connecticut. She works for Communities in Schools, a program designed to help children to stay in school. Sheila and Bruce have two children, Jae'Mie and Justin.

As for Billy Jr., he shared his father's love for music. In 1981 he graduated from Shenandoah College and Conservatory of Music in Winchester, Virginia. Billy's major was Music in Jazz Studies. Billy pursued his dream of becoming a drummer.

After playing with local jazz bands, Billy was invited to New York to serve as guest drummer for a few acts. New York City provided more positive exposure and opportunities for Billy than playing for bands locally. Eventually Billy moved to New York and joined a band called "Out of the Blue." About two years after moving to New York, he was recognized by Modern Drummer magazine as one of the city's top jazz drummers. He was part of an elite group of drummers who were called for live and studio work throughout New York City, Japan and Europe.

In 1990 Billy married Renee Rosnes, a fellow musician. A Canadian, Renee studied classical piano at the University of Toronto and moved to New York City in 1986 to pursue a career in jazz. Aside from leading their own bands, Billy and Renee have performed and recorded with such great musicians as Joe Henderson, Bobby Hutcheson, Sony Rollins, Wayne Shorter and

Billy's wedding day in 1990. (Left to right): Renee, Billy, me, and Bill.
Photo from the author's collection.

Sharing a laugh with Bill on our first wedding anniversary, 1983.
Photo from the auhtor's collection.

Wynton Marsalis, among many other artists. They perform all over the world.

In 1983, while taking a physical, Bill learned that he had a silent heart attack about three years before we were married. He retired immediately, after serving more than thirty years in the Sheriff's Department.

I decided to retire early, also. I had fulfilled my parents' prophesy of becoming a teacher, all of our children were grown, and I just wanted to spend quality time with Bill. In 1984, twenty years after beginning my teaching career, I retired from the Newport Public School System, where I had gone from a student teacher to an elementary school principal. By now my staff and students had dubbed me, "Mrs. D," and it hurt saying good-bye to them. But it was time to move on.

A family of musicians.
Bill playing the saxophone

Renee is a noted jazz pianist.

Billy, playing the drums in 1990, is an accomplished drummer and was
voted Best Jazz Drummer of the Year by *Modern Jazz* magazine.
All photos from the author's collection

Bill and I devoted our time to traveling throughout the United States and abroad. We went to Hawaii, the Bahamas, San Francisco, and Canada, and we took a cruise to the Virgin Islands. Just about every year we spent a week in Bill's hometown of Pleasantville, New Jersey. We visited Bruce and Sheila to spend time with our grandchildren. We also visited our sons and other relatives throughout the United States, too. Our marriage was filled with true happiness.

When I was home, I stayed active by taking tap dance and piano lessons. I became more active in the Newport News Alumnae Chapter of Delta Sigma Theta Sorority and served as president from 1986 to 1988. And, I put my "hands of a teacher" to work during the summers teaching Vacation Bible School at my church, Carver Memorial Presbyterian Church in Newport News.

In 1993 I began to notice that Bill was not as active and

After retiring I became more active in the Newport New Alumnae Chapter of Delta Sigma Theta Sorority. I am in the first row, second from the right. *Photo from the author's collection*

required more frequent visits to the doctor. I became a bit more selective about foods. The doctor advised me to eliminate liver from our diet and to eat low sodium, low fat, low cholesterol foods. He also suggested that we cut down on sweets. Bill would jokingly remark that he was always happy when company came because then he would get "good home cooking."

In 1994 Bill cut back on his beloved lawn work, hiring others to help him. Although he went to the doctor regularly, I noticed that he was losing weight. I began going to the doctor with him. On one visit I was informed that Bill was experiencing heart failure. I was shocked! He and I were doing all that the doctor recommended. I couldn't understand why his condition was worsening. I refrained from talking with Bill too much about his condition, although he knew that the doctor had explained it to me in detail.

Visiting my sisters and brother in 1990. (Left to right):
Lillian, Buddy, me, and Lillie.

All ready for my tap dance performance in 1989.
Photo from the author's collection

In early November, 1994 Bill had a massive heart attack. He died on November 13, 1994 nearly 12 years after our wedding. I was heartbroken. I did not expect him to die so early. He had been such a good husband!

Missing Bill tremendously, I found it difficult to live in our home in Newport News. In October, 1996 I decided to move back to my home in Hampton, where I had raised Dickie. There, I began using my "hands of a teacher" to write this book.

•

Epilogue

F requently, I have been asked, "How do you feel now that you are a teacher?'

My reply was always the same, "I feel just the same as I felt when I was working on the farm. I have been blessed and I am thankful!"

Thankful for my parents who instilled a dream in me. I will never forget the day they pulled me aside and said, "Freda, we are going to make a teacher out of you." They always supervised homework, motivating me to set high standards and to work hard to achieve my goals.

Thankful for people like Georgetta Manley, Dr. Martha Dawson, Dr. Mary Christian, and Dr. Marion Vassar, who saw more potential in me than I ever dreamed! In this world of selfish people, it's refreshing to meet people who reach out to pull some-one else up, rather than trying to keep people down.

Thankful for my family and friends, like the Daughtry family and the Lawtons, who were willing to make tough sacrifices.

Thankful for the academic and professional opportunities that enabled me to develop my hands into those of a teacher. Unlimited opportunities await those who refuse to give up the pursuit of their goals.

Thankful for all the co-workers and children who enriched my life and taught me valuable lessons. This proves that by humbling ourselves we can learn from everybody.

Thankful that I committed myself to the challenge of writing *Hands of A Teacher*. Through my experiences I want readers to see it matters not from whence you come.

It took me twenty-two years to achieve my childhood dream of becoming a teacher. Making my dreams a reality was challenging, enjoyable and exciting. Yet it was also tiring and time consuming. I am glad I hung in there! If I can do it, you can too!

•

Bibliography

Golier Encyclopedia. Doubleday, Dorana and Company, New York, NY, 1961.

The Bible. Kings James Version.

Jester, Annie Lash. *Newport News, Virginia: 1607-1960.* City of Newport News, VA, 1960-1961.

A Teacher
Do you have hands of a teacher?

About The Author

Alfreda "Freda" L. A. Drummond was born on May 11, 1924 on a farm in eastern, North Carolina near the town of Tarboro. She is the middle child of nine children born to Arterway and Lillie Willis Lane, who were sharecroppers.

At an early age, Freda's parents noticed that she always showed a great desire for school work, especially reading. Arterway and Lillie owned a book, which showed different shapes of hands and listed the occupations the hands represented. One day they pulled Freda aside and compared her hands to those that represented a teacher. "Your hands are shaped like the hands of a teacher. We are going to make a teacher out of you," they announced. Their statement was crystallized in young Freda's mind.

Freda grew up sharecropping on farms with her parents and siblings. When she was thirteen her mother died of pneumonia. Determined to fulfill her parents' vision for her, Freda excelled in school.

In 1942 everything looked promising for Alfreda. She graduated as class valedictorian and was awarded a full academic college scholarship to Hampton Institute in Hampton, Virginia. But as fate would have it, her father became ill with a virus shortly before she was to enroll in college causing her have to go to work to help support her family. Freda's plan was to work for a year or two before enrolling in college to pursue her dream of becoming a teacher. Unbeknown to Freda, it would be twenty-two more years before the "hands of a teacher" prophecy would be fulfilled.

In 1964, "hands of a teacher" became a reality after earning a degree in Elementary Education from Hampton Institute. Freda was hired to teach in the Newport News Public School System. She went on to become an Assistant Principal and Principal. She also completed graduate courses at the College of William and Mary, Old Dominion University, and the University of Virginia. While working towards a Master's Degree from Indiana University, the university president awarded her a certificate of honor for academic excellence in 1968.

Freda became an active member of the local, state, and national teaching and principal associations. Her professional affiliations include memberships in the National Association of Elementary School Principals, the American Association of University Women, Delta Sigma Theta Sorority, and several honor societies including Alpha Kappa Mu, Kappi Delta Pi, and Pi Lambda Theta.

Freda also served her community as a board member of the YWCA and the Girls Club. She has also been an active supporter of her church, Carver Memorial Presbyterian Church.

The recipient of numerous citations for her professional achievements, Freda resides in Hampton, Virginia. A retired teacher and principal, she has inspired many by making "hands of a teacher" a reality. Presently, she serves as a volunteer in the Newport News Public School System.

●

Order Form

Copies of this book may be purchased for $14.95 plus $3.00 shipping and handling fee for each book. (Virginia residents add 4.5% sales tax)

Please send _____copies of Hands Of A Teacher: The Alfreda Drummond Story to:

Name_____

Address_____

City_____Sate_____Zip Code_____

Enclosed is a check for $_____
Make checks payable to: *Hands Of A Teacher*

Send order form to:
      Hands Of A Teacher
      c/o Publishing Connections
      P. O. Box 1387
      Yorktown, VA 23692-1387